No Nonsense Gardening Guide™

LANDSCAPING FOR BEAUTY

By the Editors of Garden Way Publishing

Longmeadow Press

LANDSCAPING FOR BEAUTY

Prepared for Longmeadow Press by Storey Communications, Inc.

President: M. John Storey
Executive VP, Administration: Martha M. Storey
Publisher: Thomas Woll
Series Editor: Benjamin Watson

Cover and inside design by Leslie Morris Noyes
Edited by Sarah Magee
Production by Carol Jessop, Joan Genova, Judy Eliason,
and Nancy Lamb
Illustrations by Cynthia Locklin, Elayne Sears,
and Alison Kolesar

The name Garden Way Publishing is licensed to Storey
Communications, Inc., by Garden Way, Inc.

Cover photograph © Jerry Howard/Positive Images

CONTENTS

THE NO NONSENSE LIBRARY

NO NONSENSE GARDENING GUIDES

Flowering Houseplants
The Successful Vegetable Garden
Using Annuals & Perennials
Landscaping for Beauty
Herbs the Year Round
The Weekend Gardener

OTHER NO NONSENSE GUIDES

Car Guides
Career Guides
Cooking Guides
Financial Guides
Health Guides
Legal Guides
Parenting Guides
Photography Guides
Real Estate Guides
Study Guides
Success Guides
Wine Guides

Chapter 1

Designing the Home Landscape

Landscaping produces a yard and property that is beautiful, admirable, manageable, and useful. In this chapter, we'll talk about overall considerations in designing the home landscape. These include evaluating your property and your needs and drawing up a master landscaping plan.

Analyzing an Existing Landscape

Some of the common problems in existing landscapes include proportion, inappropriate plants, sparse or disfigured landscapes, disagreeable views, and plant and other hazards. Successful landscaping begins with standing back from the existing landscape and analyzing it. Does the front yard look like a jungle? Is there nothing of interest to look at? Do some plants look as if they are dying? Are too many plants all growing together? Does one large tree dominate everything? Are all of the plants you look at evergreens with small or inconspicuous fruits or flowers that don't lend color to the landscape? Are you dealing with a new property that has not been landscaped?

Proportion

What causes landscapes to look "wrong" more quickly than any other feature is plants that are out of proportion—either too big or too small. They may be out of proportion with the house, with other plants in the immediate landscape, or even with plants in surrounding landscapes.

This out-of-proportion problem is most obvious with plants that have been placed close to the house in the typical foundation planting. A foundation planting consists of trees or shrubs designed to hide the foot or more of exposed foundation readily seen above the soil line around the bottom of older homes. (Few new houses need foundation plantings, since modern building techniques have generally eliminated raised and exposed foundations.)

Proportion problems are also common with shade or evergreen trees that were planted in the yard in front of the house and have grown too large to fit the landscape.

Inappropriate Plants

A more subtle visual problem occurs when plants fail to fit a particular landscape situation, such as the use of plants whose form or texture does not complement the house's architectural style or even surrounding plants. There may be unpleasant color contrasts between different plants that bloom at the same time or between the color of the house and the plants.

Plants may also be undesirable in certain locations because of inappropriate characteristics. Fruit trees, for example, are seldom appropriate for front yards or for the living area in backyards, because falling fruit creates a mess around the tree that must be cleaned up. A similar problem is created by trees with large leaves that drop in the fall and are slow to decompose and cumbersome to rake up. In cases such as these, there is generally little that can be done except to remove the plant(s) if the maintenance work that is required is impractical.

Formal Design

Formal designs impose a very rigid appearance on the house and plants, and can increase plant maintenance if the plants must be constantly pruned or sheared to keep their artificially symmetrical shape. Examples of formal design include symmetrical, or "mirror-image," groupings of plants in the foundation planting in front of a house; many plants pruned or sheared into rigid shapes; or soldierlike straight-line plantings in a foundation planting or to form a hedge or screen.

Maintaining plants in their natural forms with correct height-reduction pruning can greatly decrease maintenance work. Where plants have been placed in straight-line fashion, adding or moving a few plants so that they are in less formal groupings can easily soften the effect. If the straight-line planting is the typical row of evergreens, include groupings of a second, more colorful plant (frequently a flowering deciduous shrub).

The Clutter Factor

For anyone who likes plants, it is easy to create an undesirable and cluttered-looking landscape because of one's inclination to add new plants. Soon your landscape no longer resembles a home environment, but looks more like a mini-arboretum.

If you are inclined to collect plants, you can select a special place in a low-visibility area for your collection. Generally, plantings in the front of the house should be kept to a minimum of three or four species that are used in groupings of at least three or five plants. Wherever possible, repeat one or more of the species to help give continuity to your design.

If a plant from your collection does especially well, you might consider moving it before it gets too large to a higher-visibility area for use as an *accent* or *focal plant*. If the plant is a shrub or perennial, try to buy or propagate additional plants so that a grouping can be used.

A Sparse or Disfigured Landscape

One of the major visual problems in many landscapes is just the opposite of clutter — it's the lack of things to look at. All too many landscapes seem to be dominated by evergreens, which don't offer the seasonal variation that adds interest to the scenery.

There are many causes of disfigured landscapes. If a lawn area has been heavily trafficked or used as a ballfield by children, portions of the turf may be reduced or nonexistent. Trees or shrubs may be damaged or disfigured from storms, diseases, insects, or human abuse. Look over all existing trees and shrubs for signs of these problems.

Hazards

Plants can present hazards. One of the most obvious exists where plants have grown large and block or obscure something, such as the house's street number. Another hazard is large plants at the end of a driveway or on the edge of the street. These may obscure a motorist's view when backing out of a driveway or pulling into traffic. Those little shrubs that were planted on either side of the driveway fifteen years ago may now be the cause of a serious accident.

Plants create another type of hazard when they interfere with utility lines. The two most common examples are street tree branches growing into overhead power lines and tree roots growing into water and sewer lines. Often, these nuisance trees must be removed.

DAMAGE FROM CLIMBING PLANTS

Another problem to look out for is damage from the roots of climbing vines growing into tree bark (which can cause the tree to starve), the wood of buildings, or even the mortar of masonry walls. To stop this damage, it is better to sever vines from their roots and let the vines die before pulling them away from the trees or structures they are attached to.

7

Before any trees are planted you should look up to see what they might interfere with in the future. You should also call the utility companies and ask them to come flag where water and sewer lines run. Trees, other plants, and even structures should be kept a considerable distance from these underground lines. Other items to avoid blocking include storm sewers, hydrants, traffic signs, utility meters, and—for those in rural locations—septic systems, leach fields, and wells.

DESIGNING THE NEW LANDSCAPE

Now it's time to put your landscape analysis on paper.

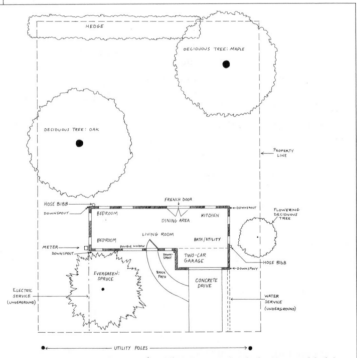

Figure 1-1. A "base plan" of your landscape, derived from the original scale drawing you did of the property, will be necessary before renovation work can begin. You may want to do a rough sketch first, then redraw it as neatly as possible to create a master base plan. It should show all the features of the site, home, and property: large landscape elements (big trees, a sizable hedge), where the roof and/or gutters drain; location of utility services (both above and underground): permanent features such as driveways, paths, fences; and how rooms are used on the first floor of the house.

CREATE A SCALE DRAWING

First, see if you have a survey plat (a scaled map showing actual or proposed features) of your property. If so, you can scale it up (draw it larger), so that you can put all of your analysis and observations on paper. If an actual plat isn't available, a legal description outlining the boundaries should be.

If no scaled plat is available, buy or borrow a measuring tape at least 50 feet long, but preferably 100 feet long for a large property. Measure your property boundary using whatever markings or features you are sure of.

Next, measure the exterior dimensions of your house and how it is located on the property, then draw the house to scale on the property. Use a large enough scale (1 inch = 10 or 20 feet

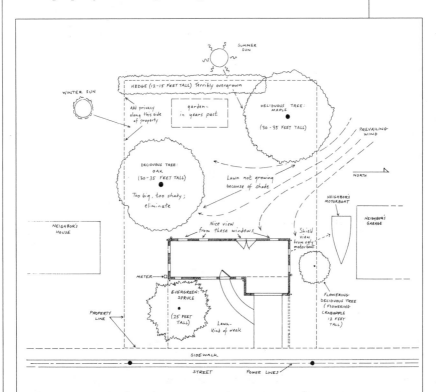

Figure 1-2. The master base plan is further enhanced by the addition of landscape features that may not be immediately apparent: how high have trees/plants grown; how do the properties abutting yours affect your landscape, if at all; what is the direction of prevailing winds, and how does the sun fall at different times of the year; are there any significant slopes or grades; and are there any views worth considering?

may be adequate), so that you have plenty of room on the paper to record both house and landscape details. It is easier to draw to scale if you use a scale ruler or draw on graph paper where you can count squares for certain footages. Be sure to record the scale you are using (1 inch = 10 feet; 1 square = 2 feet; etc.).

Draw a "base plan" of your site, including all the features of the site, home, and property, as shown in Figure 1-1. Show any fences and walls, being especially careful to note any land between a fence or wall and a neighbor's property line. Do the same for less permanent structures or features, such as above-ground movable pools, dog pens, clotheslines, children's play equipment, vegetable gardens, and compost piles.

Now draw on your property/house plan (or on separate overlays) any structural elements that will be changed and all existing vegetation, regardless of its status or condition. Show the actual spread of each plant, even if they overlap, and record the height of all trees and shrubs. Then note the approximate ages and conditions of all existing plants. Do not at this point make decisions as to what stays or gets moved or removed. Figure 1-2 is an example of how such a plan would look on a single sheet of paper (that is, without overlays).

Here is a summary of what you should put on your scale drawing:

- Property lines, noting city easements.
- House location and its exterior outline.
- Placement of doors and windows on the first floor, noting height of windows above ground, showing directions in which doors swing or slide, and noting any other important details.
- Label first-floor rooms in the house.
- Utility locations and where they attach to the house, and utility meters.
- Sidewalks, driveways, paths, patios, decks, detached garages, storage buildings, and other permanent structures; fences and walls, pools, dog pens, play areas, vegetable gardens, etc., that will not change in location.
- Note important site details, such as slope, wind direction, and views. Do this also for bordering properties. Be sure to indicate compass directions.
- Structural items and areas that can or will change, and all existing landscape plants with notes about their approximate ages and conditions.

These items will serve as the basis from which you can plan and draw a new and more elaborate landscape plan.

DEVELOPING A FINAL PLAN

Using the overlay or plan on which you have indicated all existing plants, decide and indicate which plants are definitely being removed and disposed of, based on the information gained from your earlier analysis of the landscape. Repeat this step with the plan or overlay showing any structures or paving

ENERGY CONSERVATION

The following is a list of some of the major uses of plants for energy conservation.

■ Plant large deciduous trees on the south, southwest, and west sides of houses, patios, decks, and outdoor recreation areas for summer shade.

■ Plant deciduous vines on supports or trellises against walls on the south, southwest, and west sides to again provide summer shade. These vines can also have an insulating effect in winter.

■ Plant evergreen or deciduous shrubs to shade all but the northern side of air-conditioning units.

■ Plant evergreens close to your house on the northwest side (and/ or northeast, depending upon prevailing winds) to create a dead space and insulate against winter winds.

■ Plant staggered double rows (if space permits) of tall evergreen shrubs or trees on the northwest (or northeast) side of the house to block or divert the winter wind and to control drifting snow.

■ Plant tree and shrub groups to direct the wind in desirable directions allowing cold air to settle downhill whenever possible.

■ Plant trees and shrubs to intercept the light and heat bouncing up from light-colored paved surfaces.

that can be moved or removed. These can now serve as guides for work that can be started while you are developing your final plan.

Next, develop a plan or overlay that shows what of the existing landscape you hope to maintain (even if renewal pruning is needed), and what you would like to use if it can be moved to an appropriate location. Do not, in your desire to save existing plants, impose any compromises on your design that may prove to be unsatisfactory in the future, just for the sake of saving a plant or two.

You should also never assume that just because an area was once planted it should be replanted. When in doubt, leave an area unplanted for several months, and then decide if a replacement is really necessary.

Compare this "to-stay" plan with the sketches you have done of a "future" landscape plan. Make any adjustments that are necessary to fit the two plans together. Then draw a final plan or overlay, which shows the final landscape drawn to scale, with all plants and structures in their final locations.

Selecting New Plants

At this point, no specific plants should be named on your plan other than those that are already in the landscape. The selection of new plants to add to your landscape should be a process in reverse. First design a functional area, then decide on the amount of maintenance you're willing and able to handle. Next, find the types of plants with specific characteristics that will suit these criteria (for example, a spring-flowering tree with a maximum height of 25 feet, a spreading groundcover that tolerates light foot traffic, or an evergreen shrub for background that can be maintained in natural form to 3 feet).

Make a list of plants with the various characteristics you prefer (mature height, maintenance requirements, flowering or evergreen), and compare that with lists of plants suitable to your specific site. Visit garden centers, nurseries, parks, and other places that display plants to see what the plants look like before you make your final choice. Drive through neighborhoods to see how the plants look in actual landscapes. If you cannot find the plants you've chosen at your local nursery, your nearest botanic garden may be able to suggest a source or your garden center may be able to special-order them.

Establishing a Time Frame

At this point the various components of your landscape renovation may have you a bit overwhelmed as to how to proceed. They may also have you wondering whether you can afford to improve your landscape. The best thing to do now is to develop both a renovation calendar and a renovation budget and to proceed as time and money permit.

The following is a good timetable:

1. Remove plants that will not be saved, rejuvenated, or moved.

2. Renovate or rejuvenate plants that will stay in place.

3. Move any existing plants that can be saved and used in other locations.

4. Install nonplant improvements such as paving, fencing, pools,

TIPS ON PLANNING TO DECREASE MAINTENANCE

- Install plants in groups in well-outlined, mulched beds rather than as solitary placements in the middle of a lawn.
- Use curved and flowing lines for planting areas rather than sharp corners, which can be difficult to mow around.
- Use groundcovers and mulched areas in place of lawn to decrease mowing maintenance.
- Install irrigation systems wherever possible to provide regular watering in an easier and more efficient way.
- Use perennial plants in place of annual plants, or use a combination of annuals and perennials in flower beds.
- To obtain screening or privacy, use structural materials (walls, fencing) in place of, or in combination with, plant material, to avoid the demanding maintenance of total plant screens like hedges.
- Use high-quality construction materials and plants.
- To reduce lawn wear and compaction problems, install permanent paving wherever paths have worn (or where they may develop).
- Install pads for, or mulch under, items such as seats, tables, and trash cans to ease lawn maintenance around these areas.

and structures. This would also be a good time to do any house renovation work, such as adding a room or painting the exterior.

5. Select and install all new plants that you'll be adding to your landscape plan.

6. Renovate the lawn and groundcover areas.

Add an estimated cost to each of the above. The first parts of the renovation calendar and budget — removing, rejuvenating, and/or moving existing plants — are generally the least expensive. These initial steps will prepare the landscape for the installation of new plants and features: Make them a priority, because waiting to remove, move, or prune plants and other items until after work has started may damage new plants or detract from new landscaping efforts.

If your budget is limited, these first steps may be all you can accomplish initially, but it may surprise you to see how much better a landscape can look with nothing more than a few dead or declining plants removed and a few overgrown plants pruned back to a natural, manageable size.

If you need to put in nonplant improvements right away, try to concentrate them in the front of the property or in areas of greatest use or need at the top of your list. Do likewise with the addition of plant material. It is probably more important to plant a tree this year that can begin to grow and shade the house than to add a flower garden for enjoyment and cutting.

Stretching the Landscape Budget

There are many ways to stretch your landscaping budget. The following is a list of money-saving ideas to consider.

- Buy the smallest size plants that will still be effective.

- Smaller-sized trees and shrubs suffer from less root loss if field-dug, and, therefore, begin to regrow at a faster rate than larger shrubs and trees. (Even consider buying small plants, potting them up into larger-sized containers and feeding and watering them heavily for one growing season to force some fast growth before planting them in your landscape.)

- For deciduous trees and shrubs, buy bare-rooted rather than balled-and-burlapped (B&B) or container-grown plants whenever possible.

- Use fast-growing plants for short-term effects — or as substitutes, while slower-growing plants are getting established in your landscape.

- Use smaller- or lesser-grade roses and bulbs and encourage rapid growth with good cultural practices.

- Use proven standard cultivars and varieties rather than new cultivars or introductions that are more expensive or that may not have been thoroughly tested in your area.

- Use inexpensive, fast-growing deciduous shrubs in place of fencing or walls for a less expensive screen.

- Fit your design to the existing topography rather than attempting extensive regrading.

TIPS FOR WORKING WITH A DESIGNER

- Be specific and talk freely about the type of landscape you have in mind.

- Make a list of what you want most in your yard. If mowing a lawn or harvesting your own fruit is worth the effort to you, then say so right up front.

- Be firm about what plants you don't like. If you absolutely hate ivy, then refuse to have it in your yard, no matter how perfect it is as a groundcover.

- Ask for substitutes or a second choice if the plants your designer suggests don't grab you. Your outside property should be as personalized and well thought out as your interior design — and require a lot less upkeep.

- When renovating the lawn, seed or sprig it (using small pieces of grass stems and leaves) rather than sodding it.

- Construction materials that are larger (concrete blocks) are often less expensive than smaller units (bricks).

- Propagate your own plants whenever possible.

- Use stones, bricks, or a bark mulch to pave secondary walks rather than pouring solid surfaces.

- Use annual flowers as fillers while perennials and small shrubs develop good growth.

- Use more common, less expensive plants as backgrounds for more expensive and more noticeable specimen plants.

- Use sand, gravel, or mulch as a construction base or pad rather than concrete.

- Take a chance on "bargains" for easy-to-grow plants, and

increase the plants' chances of survival with good cultural techniques.

■ Buy plants in the fall, when nurseries are clearing stock and offering lower prices.

■ Install less expensive plants first, so that an area will look planted even if it is not complete.

■ Compare prices and wait for sales. Plants, like any other consumer goods, are subject to specials and sales.

■ Space annuals, perennials, and groundcovers further apart and use larger mulched areas in between.

Whenever possible, try not to sacrifice quality for price. Landscape within your budget: Use smaller, good-quality plants, which are more likely to grow than larger, cheaper plants that may have been poorly treated and that will be less likely to reestablish successfully.

CHAPTER 2
PLANNING A NEW LANDSCAPE

JUDGING THE INITIAL LANDSCAPE

Many town and municipal building codes require that land-scaping be installed for all new house construction. Minimal landscaping budgets generally result in the use of common, inexpensive plants, which are put into designs that reflect very little thought. One small shade tree stuck in the middle of the front yard (often right in the sight line of the front door) and five or six evergreens in a row across the front of the house are typical. In an effort to gain an instant "mature" look, builders often use fast-grow-

To make a new home more attractive to prospective buyers, a "quick" landscape is often installed. Such a landscape would be overplanted with poor-quality evergreen shrubs, the lawn would be sparse and unattractive, and occasional specimen trees would be thoughtlessly placed.

ing species of plants placed too close together. The result is a landscape that looks overgrown and uncoordinated when it is not more than a few (often less than five) years old.

A shade tree placed in an aesthetically enhancing location where it may also favorably modify the environment, plus a few good-quality, high-interest shrubs constitute a far better start than the situation described above. Homeowners need to be as demanding about the landscape as they are about the interior details of their homes.

If you must have a mature look from the start, use larger plants in smaller numbers. They should be installed and spaced so as to give a finished appearance, but one that will accommodate some additional growth.

A far better solution, however, is to invest in small, good-quality, often slower-growing or dwarf plants, spaced so that 10

17

to 15 years later the landscape will look mature. In doing this, a minimal amount of maintenance each year will help to slow down the rate at which an overgrown landscape could develop. You can use temporary plants such as annuals, perennials, or groundcovers to fill the large open spaces for the first few years.

CUSTOM LANDSCAPE DESIGNS

Many nurseries and garden centers offer custom landscape designs that are available as handouts or fact sheets. Each fact sheet features a different basic architectural house style and comes with a scaled landscape drawing and plant list.

Although this may be an inexpensive way for a contractor or homeowner to obtain a landscape plan, several potential problems should be kept in mind. One of the most obvious is that using a "canned" plan creates a "copycat" and, often, a dull landscape.

Most of these prepared plans offer only one plant suggestion for each planting area that is designated; they frequently overuse evergreens at the expense of color and textural variation. You can alleviate this problem somewhat by substituting different plants from those recommended, while sticking to the basic plan.

Many prepared plans are drawn predominantly with straight-line beds and straight lines of plants. Landscapes are not only more pleasing and interesting to view, but also easier to maintain, when curved lines are used. In addition, with straight rows of plants, it is far more obvious if one plant dies or has a different growth rate than when the plants are spaced in nonlinear groups.

In general, the prepared plans do not suggest what size plant to buy (a 1-gallon versus a 3-gallon shrub, a 3-foot versus a 1-inch caliper tree, etc.), nor do they tell you how many years it will take plants of a particular size to reach maturity or to grow to the size shown on the plan. The plans generally show plants touching or overlapping, and this is not a good condition for the beginning landscape, because major maintenance will become necessary almost immediately after planting.

SAVING TREES IN NEW HOME PLANNING

Homeowners generally pay much more for a "wooded" lot than for one that is treeless. A higher price may be justified, as long as the homeowner is realistic about which plants are to be saved, and as long as the contractor makes a concerted effort to minimize damage to the plants that have been designated as worth saving.

Preserving the root environment of the trees to be saved should be a top priority. Where the root zone must be tampered with, you should take precautions prior to construction to minimize any disturbances. Keep in mind that the competition (for water, nutrients, and sun) that exists between trees in a wooded environment has restricted their root systems in comparison to their successful counterparts growing in less competitive, more open landscape situations. When wooded areas are opened up and trees thinned out, the trees left in place may have root systems less able to adapt to the new, more stressful conditions in which they are then expected to grow.

In most cases a few large trees will be saved, and the small trees will be marked for removal. Often this is the reverse of what should be done, because the large trees may be old and declining, while some of the smaller specimens may grow into excellent trees with a bit of judicious clearing and pruning. Young trees will almost always adapt to environmental changes better and more readily than older trees of the same species. In addition, young trees will be easier to remove and replace at a later time should the need arise after construction.

Trees to be saved should be physically separated from the grading and building process as much as possible. This can be done by putting a fence several feet away from the trunks to prevent equipment and supplies from touching the trees. In addition, attempts to add or remove soil should be discouraged, as should activities that compact the soil over tree roots. All of these factors can cause trees to die.

Signs of tree stress caused by construction can include premature fall coloration and leaf drop, reduced leaf size, increased twig dieback, increased or sudden susceptibility to insects and diseases, sucker growth on large branches and the trunk, and "stagheading," or the death of large scaffold branches, which results in random large branches standing dead in a tree's crown. Depending on the type and extent of environmental changes and tree injury, these signs may either show up soon after the damage has occurred or reveal themselves slowly over an extended period of time.

Plant Selection and Care for a New Landscape

Poor coordination of plant species with the existing environmental conditions causes many plants added to a new landscape to die. Landscapers often fail to note the environmental conditions — soil type, pH, moisture-holding capacity and drainage, amount of sun and shade, and prevailing wind direction — of the finished site. Each site has its own microclimate, and plants should be selected accordingly.

Plants that may thrive in an established neighborhood, where the soil has been rehabilitated over time and where tall trees lend a degree of shade, may simply die on a new site only one block away, where the topsoil was removed and no trees were left standing. Some plants will survive virtually any environmental conditions, but the conditions found at most new building sites are rarely conducive to healthy plant growth, and the cheap, fast-growing plants that are quickly put in to finish most jobs will struggle to survive.

Even if plants are properly installed in a new landscape, they may quickly deteriorate because no provisions are made for follow-up maintenance. The person hired to plant the plants did just that — planted them. With luck, the plants were at least watered and mulched to help them get started. But what if no rain falls after the landscape is installed? Was anyone hired to come back and follow up on the planting job with some form of routine maintenance, which might amount to no more than a once-a-week deep watering? Probably not, and therefore, even if the best quality plants were installed using the best planting techniques, the failure of someone to simply water the plants may kill the new landscape. This is especially true if the landscape is installed in late spring or during the summer, when the environment is likely to be the most stressful.

Do a Scale Drawing

In light of all these problems, what should the new homeowner do?

The best approach is probably to treat the brand-new landscape like any landscape needing renovation. As described in Chapter 1, start by doing a scale drawing of the property, house, site details, and any plants that have been saved or added to the landscape. Do not draw the plants to their present size, but to a mature size or a size they could be expected to attain 10 to 15 years from now. That will give a better indication of how quickly the plants may outgrow their location, or whether they can be used as they presently exist.

CHAPTER 3

CREATING A HEALTHY LAWN

The way to have a beautiful lawn is to get a good grasp on what a *healthy* lawn is and how to keep it that way. In this chapter, you'll find basic ideas and procedures to keep your lawn healthy and gorgeous.

THE SOIL

The foundation of a healthy lawn is healthy soil. A healthy soil allows air, water, nutrients, and roots to move through it easily. It holds water like a sponge, yet permits excess water to drain away before the grass drowns. It is alive with microorganisms, worms, and other beneficial life-forms, which work constantly on minerals (rocks) and decaying matter, breaking them down into solutions that are essential for plant nutrition.

If you were to take a side view of the soil under your lawn, you would probably see two distinct layers. Above is the *topsoil*, usually somewhat loose and dark; under that is the *subsoil*, often hard and claylike, or coarse and sandy. Grass can grow in this subsoil, but weeds fare much better.

Dig into your soil and see where the shovel hits the subsoil. If you have at least 5 to 6 inches of topsoil under the lawn, you're in good shape. If not, you could always pull up the lawn and add more, but that's not a job most people are interested in doing. With some patience, though, you can rehabilitate the soil you have, and at the same time transform some of the subsoil into real topsoil.

The major differences between topsoil and the subsoil beneath it are the amount of *humus*, or organic matter, it contains, and the size of the rock particles in it. A good topsoil consists of from 3 to 10 percent humus; a subsoil might have 1 percent or less. To turn your subsoil into real soil, you're going to have to find a way to get more humus and soil life into it. Using the information below, you can create your own humus right under your lawn.

One very simple way to immediately improve your soil is through the use of a soil conditioner. This will temporarily improve the soil structure while you work at building up a healthy soil. Soil conditioners will help break up the heavier, compacted soils, as well as improving the moisture-holding capacity of sandy soils. The better organic soil conditioners also add soil nutrients, which unlock soil elements and help speed up the formation of a good living soil from a poor one. Once your

BENEFITS OF GOOD SOIL STRUCTURE

- Improved soil aeration. Water drains quickly and doesn't sit in the root zone; therefore, roots develop strongly and quickly, soil life flourishes, and the likelihood of soil-borne diseases diminishes.

- Good structure means less compaction from foot traffic, because the soil doesn't stay wet.

- Good soil warms up faster, seeds sprout faster, and plants grow faster.

- No dry spots. With good structure, water is retained.

- Improved nitrogen release, because soil microbes can work on decaying matter. Also, nitrogen doesn't drain away.

- Better weed control. Many weeds only sprout in very wet or very dry soil. And the superior lawn that a good soil structure produces will crowd out weeds, too.

- Less erosion. Water penetrates and soil doesn't wash away, because the granules are bonded together.

- Increased fertility. A living soil converts minerals and organic matter into nutrients safely and almost endlessly.

soil has become full of life and has the proper structure, it can be easily maintained with basic natural lawn care practices, as discussed below. With a good soil, plus proper mowing and watering, your lawn problems will be few.

FERTILIZING

Is it really necessary to fertilize lawns? For most homeowners, the answer is yes. But if you have a well-structured soil, full of worms and other soil life, and you can leave most of your clippings to decompose, then your fertilizer needs will be minimal. Think of fertilizing as soil building instead of plant feeding. Natural fertilizers will increase soil life, improve structure, and provide nutrients.

Is it better to use synthetic chemical or natural fertilizers? Natural fertilizers break down slowly to provide long-term nutrition and steady rather than excessive growth. They also encourage soil life and help build better soil structure. A few of the better natural fertilizer blends contain additional beneficial bacteria and enzymes, so the soil will come back to life more quickly. These superior fertilizers often provide *trace elements,* vital nutrients that plants need in minute quantities. It is almost impossible to harm a lawn with natural fertilizers. Though sometimes more expensive

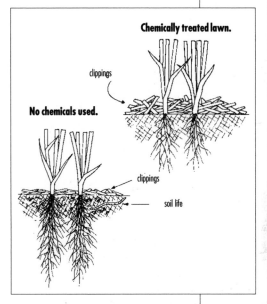

Chemically treated lawn.

clippings

No chemicals used.

clippings

soil life

than chemical fertilizers, natural fertilizers are, in the long run, quite economical.

Synthetic chemical fertilizers act more quickly than natural fertilizers, and they are often less expensive. But chemical fertilizers have many drawbacks. They release their nutrients too quickly, creating excessive top growth before the roots can catch up. This kind of growth weakens the grass. Much of a quickly released fertilizer tends to get leached away, especially on sandy soils. *If you use chemical fertilizers, try them in small quantities applied frequently.* This will prevent overfertilizing, prevent waste from leaching, and allow the soil to buffer harmful effects much more easily. Most chemical fertilizers can burn a lawn if it's not watered soon after application. Their high salt concentration literally sucks moisture from the grass plants.

pH Testing

When a soil is tested for pH, the test will result in a number. Seven is exactly neutral, so anything below that is acid to some degree, and anything above is alkaline. Most lawn grasses seem to do best between 7.5 and 6; that is, generally neutral or slightly acid. Keeping the pH in the right range is extremely important. When you seem to be doing everything right for your lawn, but it isn't responding, have your soil tested for pH.

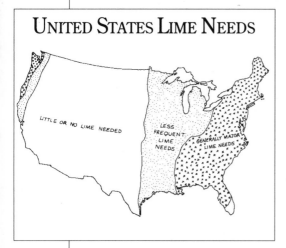

UNITED STATES LIME NEEDS

LITTLE OR NO LIME NEEDED

LESS FREQUENT LIME NEEDS

GENERALLY MAJOR LIME NEEDS

Every county of the United States has a Co-operative Extension Service that can help get your soil tested, and almost every state has a Land Grant College that tests soil as part of its responsibilities to the state. If you want to do the testing yourself, you can buy an inexpensive pH test kit or pH meter at a garden center.

Continue to add organic matter and natural fertilizers, no matter what your soil's pH is. If it's on the acid side, add ground limestone, available at any garden center. Use dolomite limestone if it's available.

Lime should be applied with a fertilizer spreader — never with your bare hands, because it can burn. The amount of lime to use depends on the type of soil you have and the degree to which you want to raise the pH. On a good loam, 70 pounds of ground limestone for every 1,000 square feet of lawn surface will raise the pH one full number. On a sandy soil, 40 to 50 pounds will raise it the same amount; very sandy soil will need even less. A heavy clay soil requires 80 to 90 pounds per 1,000 square feet to raise the pH by a factor of one.

Some experts feel that you shouldn't apply more than 75 pounds of lime per 1,000 square feet in one season, because it can lock up other soil minerals. So, if your soil is going to need a lot of lime, it might be better to divide the applications over two seasons. Early spring or fall liming (but never in contact with new grass seed) will give the best results.

If you have alkaline soil, cottonseed meal is a good acidifier as well as a fertilizer. It is found packaged in the better garden centers. Gypsum (calcium sulfate) is even more common, and less expensive. Since alkaline soil is fairly uncommon in the United States, never lower soil pH without first getting an accurate pH test.

Natural Fertilizers

The three major nutrients lawns use are nitrogen (N), phosphorus (P), and potassium (K). In terms of N-P-K, lawns generally like a 4-1-2 fertilizer. *This does not have to be exact!* Natural fertilizers may provide a 6-1-1, 2-1-1, 5-2-3, or any similar formula and still bring good results.

In addition to N-P-K, there are ten other known elements that grass needs in lesser quantities.

One is iron. Lack of iron causes chlorosis, a yellowing of new leaves. Many gardeners, seeing yellow blades, assume there is a nitrogen deficiency. But if additional nitrogen doesn't cure it, iron usually will.

Most natural fertilizers contain some of these minor nutrients. Others, especially sea products, contain many valuable trace elements — helpful substances that, though not entirely vital, will enhance plant growth in one or more ways.

When to Fertilize

When to fertilize depends on whether your lawn is composed of cool-season or warm-season grasses. Cool-season grass will best utilize fertilizer in the early fall. Fall fertilizing, before the weather turns too cold, will help stimulate root growth, and food production and storage, making for a healthier lawn next spring. Apply the fertilizer in early to mid-September, or up until mid-October, if your climate is mild. You want to give the fertilizer a chance to work before temperatures turn so cold that the soil life can't break it down into usable form.

The other time to fertilize cool-season grasses is in late spring, or about the time when the initial spurt of rapid lawn growth is beginning to slow down. Fertilizing a healthy lawn at this time is not vital, unless you plan to keep it green throughout the summer rather than letting it go dormant. Be sure to fertilize before the weather becomes hot and dry — usually in late May.

Early spring fertilizing of cool-season grass should be done only on a stunted, weak lawn that doesn't take off when it should. Give it a heavy fertilizing in late March or early April. Keep the grass cut high over the summer and fertilize heavily again in the early fall. The grass on a healthy lawn will take off without any fertilizer prompting.

Warm-season grasses should be fertilized differently from northern lawns. They do not go dormant in the summertime, but actually grow more aggressively. Cool spring and fall weather slows their growth, and the winter is their dormant time (though winter is an active time for weeds in the South).

Fertilize heavily in mid-spring as your main application. You could break fertilizing up into early and late spring applications. Fertilize lightly again in midsummer, because the grass will be using up many nutrients during its active summer growth. A schedule of April-June-August (with natural fertilizers) is safe for most warm-season grasses.

The Problem of Thatch

People have the erroneous idea that, if they leave their clippings on the lawn, these clippings will turn into thatch. That is not usually the case. Thatch is actually an interwoven mass of stolons, stems, rhizomes, roots, leaf blades, and sheaths, all sitting on top of the soil surface. Thatch has become a major lawn problem in modern-day lawns.

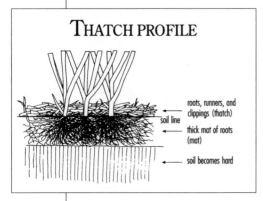

THATCH PROFILE

roots, runners, and
clippings (thatch)
soil line
thick mat of roots
(mat)

soil becomes hard

If you poke your finger down through your grass, it should go into the soil quite easily. If you find a barrier of about ½ to ¾ inch (or more) of matted grass parts, you have thatch. You'll be able to feel it. A thin layer of grass clippings is nothing to worry about.

A serious case of thatch can take years to form. Its complete removal can take years, too, but there are ways to speed the process. Whatever else you do, keep in mind the long-range intention of creating a rich, living, and porous soil, in which decomposition occurs rapidly and roots penetrate deeply. Take these steps immediately:

■ While handling a thatch problem, catch the grass clippings in a mower bag so they don't add to it.

■ Change your watering practices. Water deeply and let the thatch area get *slightly* dry. Encourage the roots to go down.

■ Core-aerate the lawn. Do this at least twice a year, in the spring and early fall. A core aerator pokes 2- to 3-inch holes into the soil (the deeper the better) and throws out the cores as it moves along. The cores eventually break down into the lawn. Without damaging a lawn, an aerator provides instant holes for air, water, fertilizer, and roots.

Go over the lawn twice, making holes 4 to 6 inches apart. Be sure to water the soil the night before, so the aerator can penetrate as deeply as possible. Rent a machine with a neighbor or two and it will be cheap. Aerating goes very fast, and it is probably one of the best things you can do for any lawn. You can aerate each September and follow immediately with a heavy fertilizing. Water afterward to get some of the fertilizer down into the soil, where the roots are supposed to be.

■ Get some *life* into the thatch layer and the soil. You shouldn't be interested in anything that will produce a lot of new growth. You want bacteria to decompose and any dead or decaying matter above ground. Any of the high-quality organic fertilizer blends will work well. Try sea products, through your hose-end sprayer. These products will also help restore life to the soil, open it up for drainage and root growth, and bring back earthworms.

It is entirely possible to rid your lawn of thatch within a two- to three-year period without mechanical removal, if you use proper natural lawn care techniques, soil conditioners, and fertilizers that contain microlife.

GRASSES

You can classify a lawn grass as either a cool-season or warm-season grass. Cool-season grasses grow best in northern climates and thrive at temperatures averaging 60° to 80°F. They will survive freezing winter temperatures, but can't take truly hot weather for long without going dormant. Often, two or more different types of cool-season grasses will grow quite well together.

Cool-season grasses can be planted over a warm-season lawn in the South as *wintergrass* to keep the lawn green during colder weather. As soon as the weather warms up, the warm-season grasses take over again.

Provided there is enough moisture, cool-season grasses will grow in most of the northern states as well as at higher elevations and in coastal areas, where temperatures are cooler. However, there are some areas in Canada and the northern plains and mountain states that are too tough or dry for a nice cool-season lawn. The grasses that will grow in these places are what are called *native grasses*. These are the same grasses that can be found growing wild on the range and the prairie.

Grasses can be *fine-bladed* (thin and fairly soft to the touch), or *coarse* (wider and rough to the touch). Most long-standing home lawns were originally intended to be fine-bladed, though the coarse types have often sneaked in and taken over. You'll notice patches of coarse grass sticking up in clumps, especially in midsummer when the other grasses might be dormant or growing very slowly.

Some lawn grasses can be grown only from sprigs, plugs,

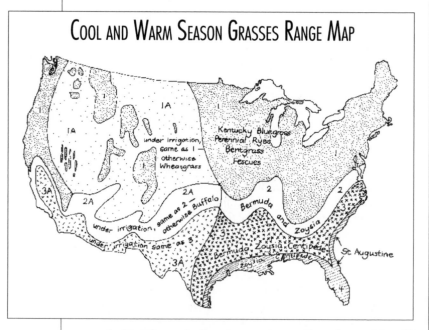

COOL AND WARM SEASON GRASSES RANGE MAP

or sod. For the majority of grass types, though, seed is still available. Typically, you will find grass seed sold as a *mixture*, a *blend*, or a *straight* type. Mixtures, two or more grass types packaged together, commonly consist of bluegrass, fescue, and annual rye. A blend consists of two or more varieties, called *cultivars*, of the same type of grass. A straight seed is exactly one type and cultivar of grass. The warm-season grasses are almost always sold as straight seed, because one of these grass types would thoroughly dominate another within the course of a season. The cool-season grasses are usually sold as mixtures.

When the time comes to choose your seed, knowledgeable nursery keepers are your best friends. They can recommend the correct prepackaged mixture, or might be able to mix a custom one for you. They'll know how to read a seed package label and will be able to tell you exactly what it means.

Don't get stuck planting the wrong type of grass! Once it's growing, grass can't easily be removed. Don't buy seed that is old or that isn't labelled. Even the loose bulk seed in hardware store bins comes in labeled sacks, so ask to see a label before buying. A store's "problem lawn" mixture might turn out to be all tall fescue and weed seed. Reputable storeowners will carry good mixes from reputable seed growers. Discount grass seed is rarely a bargain. Seed from a good nursery or garden center, even if it costs a little more, is a sound investment.

SEEDING A LAWN

Though grass seeds will sprout in hot and wet soil, these conditions are also highly conducive to weeds, insects, and disease. So do yourself a favor and hold off on seeding during the summer. Wait until the weather breaks (late August to mid-September). If you need a lawn fast, put down some pregrown grass sod.

By far the best time to seed all grass types is late August to mid-September, when the soil is nice and warm, yet the air has cooled down from summer temperatures. Weeds are not as active at this time and the soil isn't soggy, as you often find it in the spring. Mulching with straw or peat moss will hold moisture in, but will not substitute for regular watering. If you can keep the soil consistently moist without drowning the seed, germination will be quick.

Even if you are blessed with the right temperature and moisture conditions, there are still ways to mess up. *The most common mistake is using too little seed.* Another mistake is *using old seed.* If you are using older seed, make sure you sow it more heavily — maybe 1½ times the normal amount.

Using the wrong type of seed can cause untold difficulties. A sun-loving grass planted in a shady area will be a great failure. Ask the staff at your local nursery to recommend a variety for your specific lawn conditions. Every year thousands of people trust the name of the seed or the picture on the package and end up with a problem lawn.

Choosing your seed by the price tag is usually a mistake. The better lawn seeds are a little more expensive. By the pound, Kentucky bluegrass appears to be the most expensive of the common cool-season grasses, but because its seeds are so small, it turns out to be one of the cheapest. One pound of bluegrass seed covers as much area as 4 pounds of other types.

The last common seeding error is *poor soil preparation*. Without a decent soil to grow in, any seed will have a rough time of it. Take care of your soil, and it will support a beautiful lawn.

REPLACING AN EXISTING LAWN

If you are planting a lawn where an old one exists, you have to decide whether to strip off the old lawn or turn it under. A heavy-duty rototiller can break up the old lawn and mix it deeply into the soil, providing a lot of otherwise lost organic matter.

If you choose to strip the lawn off instead of going through all the labor involved in tilling it up, you'll need to rent a sod cutter. This machine makes quick work of the old lawn, peeling it off in strips about 18 inches wide.

Next you'll have to add your soil amendments and more topsoil, if it's needed. Then till everything. The soil will be fluffed up, so don't be scared if it looks too high. It will settle some, and you'll be rolling it later, too.

After rototilling, there will be mounds and dips that you must level out. You'll get fast results with a 3- or 4-foot-wide grading rake, leveling first in one direction, then the other. You can stretch a piece of string across the planting bed to determine your progress.

The next step is to *give the ground a thorough soaking*. If you have the time, keep it watered for three or more weeks. Because August is too hot and dry for seeding, it's an excellent month for this step. The purpose of the watering is to settle the soil and to encourage weeds to sprout before you seed. You can pull them, hoe every few days, or even run a tiller over them (1 to 2 inches deep at most). The soil should not be tilled too finely.

The best way to put the seed down is with a drop spreader. It will distribute evenly and not allow the wind to toss the seed around. Mix the seed up before filling the spreader, and be careful to leave an opening large enough to let the large as well as the small seeds (such as bluegrass) pass through.

Now crisscross the yard with the spreader, trying to distribute about 15 to 20 seeds per square inch. Be sure to overlap the tracks of the spreader with each pass. After the seed is down, rake it in ⅛ to ¼ inch deep with an inverted leaf rake.

If you've seeded in early September, all you need to do now is water enough to keep the soil from drying out. It would be beneficial to spread a light coat of peat moss on top of the soil, to conserve moisture and prevent water runoff. Soak it down fast so it doesn't blow away, or make it slightly moist and crumbly before you toss it on (no thicker than ½ inch). If you seeded in mid to late spring, or during the summer, the soil will need a thicker coat of peat or a covering of straw to keep the hot sun from quickly drying it out.

You can leave peat moss and finer mulches where they are; they'll soon vanish into the lawn. Rake out a straw mulch, though. Let the grass grow an inch higher than normal before cutting it, and keep it on the high side at least until mid-fall. Use a sharp mower blade and mow carefully. Remember that there are other seeds in the seed mix that will be sprouting soon, or that are just starting out.

Sod Lawns

Many people have heard that putting down sod is much more expensive than seeding a lawn. But the long-term cost difference is a lot less than the original price discrepancy. The major factors are time and water. You can water a sod lawn daily (sometimes less often) and have it fairly well established in two to three weeks; a seeded lawn might take two or three weeks of daily watering just to germinate. For the next week or two after that, the seeded lawn must not be allowed to dry out, or the young sprouts will die. Sometimes you might have to water twice a day. After that, you'll still have to keep watering as needed until the grass is firmly established.

Many people do not have access to free water. And finding time to water daily, especially when you have to move the sprinkler around to cover larger areas, is not easy.

Prepare soil for sod the same way you would prepare it for a seed lawn. Initially, sod will grow in almost any soil,

OTHER TIPS ON SOD

■ Once you have the sod at your property, do not let it dry out. If it is rolled or folded, install it within 48 hours.

■ Always make sure to keep the sod that is against walks or driveways well watered, as these places dry out fast.

■ When watering your new sod, remember not to walk on it if the ground is thoroughly saturated. You'll sink in and make a mess of your new lawn.

but it won't survive long unless the soil is rich enough to support healthy lawn growth. The sod you buy has probably been vigorously and chemically fed and treated — its shallow root system and somewhat matted form will attest to that. A rich soil planting bed will help it survive in its new home.

The main idea is to get the sod's roots to dig into the soil as quickly as possible. A speedy rooting will prevent the grass from drying out and will get it established before snows or droughts hit. *Soil moisture, as well as soil nutrients, will attract the roots downward.* If you water the sod lightly, rather than keeping the soil beneath it moist, the roots will grow into the sod rather than into the soil. You'll end up with instant thatch instead of instant lawn.

Sod should be laid out in a staggered pattern, similar to the way bricks are normally laid. The seams on the shorter side of the sod pieces should be close to the middle of the pieces above and below it. If the lawn has a slope to it, lay the sod across rather than down the slope. This will prevent water from forming channels in the seams during watering or heavy rains.

The typical home yard has a straight walkway or driveway to use as a border for your first strip. Unroll the sod along that starter strip first, then begin the next strip with a half piece of sod, so its end will line up with the middle of the first piece in your starter strip. Then continue with full pieces. Keep the seams as tight as possible, but don't overlap them.

Never stretch the sod when you lay it down — it will shrink a little when it dries out, and you'll find gaps between the seams. To cut off the ends of the sod strips, or to cut around trees or beds, use a long, sharp knife or a sharp, straight-edged spade or edging tool. These pieces come in handy for replacing the bad sections of sod that inevitably turn up as you unroll it.

When you have finished laying down the sod, give the whole lawn a good rolling with a half-full roller. This will ensure good contact with the soil, as well as tighter seams. After rolling, gently rake the top of the sod to straighten up the grass and make the seams less visible.

DISEASE PREVENTION

Aside from building the health of your soil and lawn, there are some specific ways to prevent lawn disease.

1. Most important, *plant a mixture of grasses rather than just a single variety.* Diseases can be quite selective, and a mixture of grasses will prevent the complete destruction of your lawn.

2. *Plant disease-resistant varieties.* For recommendations, check with your local nursery or with The Lawn Institute, P. O. Box 108, Pleasant Hill, TN 38578.

3. *Make sure you aren't overwatering.* If you can't keep your

Preceding page: Annual beds and borders. ANN REILLY: PHOTO/NATS. **Inset, above: Home landscaping in progress.** DAVID M. STONE: PHOTO/NATS.

Full-page photo: A tree island planting.
JERRY HOWARD/POSITIVE IMAGES. **Inset:
Removing a shrub from its container
before planting.** ANN REILLY: PHOTO/NATS.

Full-page photo: A bed can be planted around an attractive focal-point rock. JERRY HOWARD/POSITIVE IMAGES. **Inset, top: Rolls of sod.** DAVID M. STONE: PHOTO/NATS. **Inset, above: Fitting together pieces of sod.** DAVID M. STONE: PHOTO/NATS.

Full-page photo: Flowering dogwoods (*Cornus florida*). JOHN A. LYNCH: PHOTO/NATS. **Inset, above: *Magnolia soulangiana*.** ROBERT E. LYONS: PHOTO/NATS. **Inset, opposite page: Mountain-laurel (*Kalmia latifolia*).** DOROTHY LONG: PHOTO/NATS.

Full-page photo: A cottage perennial garden with peonies.
IVAN MASSAR/POSITIVE IMAGES. **Inset: A summer garden of marigolds and morning glories.** DAVID M. STONE: PHOTO/NATS.

lawn surface dry, consider drain tile or regrading. Disease is not a problem in arid regions of the country.

4. *Water sufficiently.* Underwatering a lawn, to keep it barely growing when it should either be heavily watered or allowed to go dormant, leads to disease- and insect-prone grass.

5. *Make sure there is a free flow of air.* Thin out dense shrub or tree growth to open up the yard a little.

6. *Remove thatch.* Thatch creates a humid jungle on top of the soil and helps disease proliferate. Aerating breaks through thatch and reduces soil compaction.

WEED CONTROL

Unfortunately, you cannot rid your lawn of all weeds without chemicals or hand-pulling. But you can change certain lawn conditions by improving your mowing, watering, and fertilizing habits — enough to make your lawn unacceptable to most weeds. Your lawn can reach the point at which chemical weed killers aren't needed.

The first step toward eradicating your weeds is to identify them. You can pull up a weed and carry it to an expert, such as a nursery keeper, for identification or consult a gardening reference book in your local library. Because there are many different kinds of both weeds and herbicides, it will do no good to apply a herbicide until you know it is effective on the specific type of weed you want to kill.

Once you choose a chemical, use it to spot-kill individual weed plants so you don't have to put the chemical on the weed-free portion of the lawn. Follow the manufacturer's directions carefully. Make chemicals work for you with one correct application instead of many haphazard ones.

If you have a highly weed-infested lawn, it is definitely worth your while to hire the services of lawn professionals. See if you can have your lawn treated for weeds without having it fertilized chemically at the same time. Professionals really can do a better job controlling weeds than most homeowners. If your lawn is treated in the early spring or early fall, you'll still have time to reseed after the weeds have shriveled away. Mid-summer treatments are not recommended; wait until early fall.

MOWING

Perhaps the single greatest cause of lawn distress is something most people don't even think about — mowing the grass too short. Grass is a living plant. If it is cut too short, the plant is unable to get the food and energy it needs to grow. It's more susceptible to disease and insect damage. It's weaker and less able to crowd out weeds. Many people could have much better looking lawns in a matter of weeks simply by not cutting them too short. The proper height for most lawn grasses is higher than most people are cutting now.

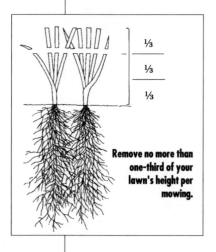

Remove no more than one-third of your lawn's height per mowing.

A general rule to follow is *never cut off more than one-third of the blade at once*. This will keep the grass from losing too much of its food factory and going into shock.

Cut grass when it's dry. A dry lawn stands up straighter and gives a cleaner cut. It is less messy, too. If the grass blades don't seem to want to dry out, you might have a problem with inadequate air flow in your yard, or too much shade. Shaded lawns should normally be cut a little higher than those in full sun, to make up for lack of sunlight.

Make your first spring cut short. This cuts away some of the dead grass left from the previous season, invigorates and stimulates the lawn, allows more sunlight to reach the newly forming blades, and helps to heat the soil. Then raise the mower height to about 2 inches and leave it there for a couple of cuts, or until the entire lawn has started to grow vigorously. Cutting at this height encourages the grass to thicken up.

When the grass really starts to take off, let it reach 3 to 4 inches in height, and keep it there. By keeping it high, you can crowd out many potential weeds, especially crabgrass.

What about grass clippings? In theory, if you were to leave all your clippings to decompose on the lawn, you would never have to fertilize, because you would simply be recycling the grass continually. Whenever you remove the clippings from a lawn, you are disrupting the natural cycle of growth and decomposition. You are removing nutrients which must somehow be replaced, or the lawn will deteriorate.

Many lawns stay green and healthy without being fertilized. Now, you may be saying to yourself, "I'm never going to fertilize again... I'll just leave the grass clippings on the lawn and let them recycle." Hold on! Before you act on that decision, there are certain adjustments to make and factors to consider.

First, the clippings must be short enough so that they do not mat down on top of the lawn. They should filter down to the soil level and quickly decompose. *Cut often* or the clippings will be too long — they'll mat up on top of the lawn and choke out the grass. If the clippings are long, you could try mowing over them again to help disperse them.

The second factor to take into account regarding lawn clippings is that, on over-chemicalized lawns, clippings may not decompose as quickly as on chemical-free lawns. Certain chemicals kill off the bacteria and microbes that aid decomposition, and make worms, the soil's intestines, scarce or nonexistent. Catch or rake up the grass clippings on a once over-chemicalized lawn until the life in the soil is restored.

The third factor concerning grass clippings is *thatch*. Clippings will add to thatch if the condition already exists. If you have a thatch problem, remove the clippings until the thatch problem is solved.

CHAPTER 4

LANDSCAPING WITH TREES AND SHRUBS

Trees and shrubs contribute more to a landscape than just beauty. They can also increase the value of a property; screen out undesirable views or accent desirable ones; increase the amount of privacy; stabilize the soil and reduce erosion; buffer noise and glare; and feed and shelter wildlife and birds, many of which eat undesirable insects. In this chapter, you'll learn how to remove and/or renovate existing trees and shrubs, how to install new ones, and how to maintain your trees and shrubs to keep them healthy.

REMOVAL OF EXISTING TREES AND SHRUBS

The first step in a landscape renovation involves removing existing plants that cannot be saved by spraying, pruning, or relocation. If you need to remove small shrubs or trees, all that may be necessary is to cut the tree trunk or shrub branches off as close to the ground as possible. Many plants will not sprout any new growth, and throwing a shovelful of soil over any exposed stems will help encourage the rotting or decomposition of the roots.

This should be adequate if no replacement plants are to be installed in the same area. If new trees and shrubs will be planted, it is best to remove both the above-ground plant and as much of its root system as possible.

Before cutting and digging out plants, you'll need to do whatever is necessary to prevent damage to neighboring plants that are to be saved. Tie branches of trees and shrubs together or up out of the way to avoid damaging them, or put some form of barrier around them. For small shrubs and other low plants, such as perennials and groundcovers, you can turn a bushel basket or trash can upside down over them to protect them.

Keep in mind that, as you dig out the root system of one plant, you may be injuring or digging out portions of neighboring root systems as well. Concentrate on removing major roots that are located directly beneath a plant to avoid injuring the roots of others. Whenever possible, get a good grip on the roots and dig them out.

If you need to remove a large tree, it is advisable to have an experienced, insured arborist do the work. Though the cost per tree may seem high, it becomes more reasonable if you consider the damage you might inflict on yourself or your house, should you insist on doing it yourself.

RENEWING TREES AND SHRUBS

There are several things you may need to do to renew trees and shrubs. The most obvious chore will be to prune those that are overgrown.

Although you may have to prune trees and shrubs that have been damaged by storms and the like soon after the damage occurs, elective pruning of most plants should take place only at certain times of the year, generally when the plants are dormant.

It's easier to prune deciduous trees and shrubs when they are without leaves, usually from late fall until early spring. This will allow you to fully evaluate the crown of the plant to determine what should be removed. With evergreens there is no such "nonleaf" period; they can be pruned at any time, although fall pruning might stimulate new growth that could be killed if it has not hardened off prior to the first freeze.

Many deciduous shrubs can be totally renewed by cutting them off at ground level and allowing a whole new crown to develop from buds on the root system. This is generally not the case with evergreens, and the severity of pruning they can withstand varies widely. A good reference should be consulted before severely pruning back any plant.

Many shrubs can be "renewal pruned" if you feel that completely removing all top growth is too severe. With renewal pruning, one-third to one-half of the shrub's stems are pruned back to the ground over two or three years, until all of the old stems have been removed and replaced by new growth. This is a way to develop an entirely new crown in a couple of years without leaving an obvious hole at the beginning. (Again, this practice is primarily restricted to deciduous shrubs.)

If the height of a tree must be reduced, remove branches that are too long back to the main branches or to the tree's trunk. If the tree has a main or central leader (giving the tree a pyramidal shape, as with many evergreen trees) there really is no way to cut back the tree's height without radically altering the shape of the tree's crown.

Pruning isn't the only way to renovate plants that you want to keep in the landscape. You may also need to treat plants for

37

disease and insect problems, or to feed them to encourage more vigorous growth. They may also need to be weeded and mulched, and put on a more even watering regimen. Adapting proper cultural practices will help to renovate or rejuvenate many plants.

Pruning

Pruning cuts should be made just outside the branch collar, which is tissue of the trunk or main branch (see Figure 4-1). Leaving the branch collar is important in wound closure, because it helps to minimize internal decay. If you are pruning diseased plants, disinfect your pruning equipment after each cut by dipping it in alcohol or a 10 percent bleach solution.

Figure 4-1. Use the branch collar as your guide when pruning (left). After the cut is made, just the collar should remain (below), not a significant stub.

On some plants you will see a second line or marking that will help direct your pruning cuts. Often a darkened line of rough bark runs from the branch bark crotch into the trunk bark. This is called the *branch bark ridge* and serves as a second pruning-cut guideline (see Figure 4-2).

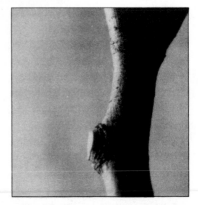

When only a portion of a branch is being removed, you generally want to make a cut that angles away from, and just slightly above, a bud headed in the direction in which you want new growth to go (see Figure 4-3). In most cases, such a cut should be above a bud that will produce a new branch and then grow out away from the center of the plant.

Whether pruning away entire main branches, or only portions of small branches, be sure to use pruning equipment that is sharp and large enough for the job. Hedge and lawn-edging

Figure 4-2. Another pruning guide is the branch bark ridge, which can be recognized by a ridge of rough, dark tissue that runs from the crotch angle into the trunk area. Make your pruning cuts outside the branch collar at a 30-to 45-degree angle to the branch bark ridge.

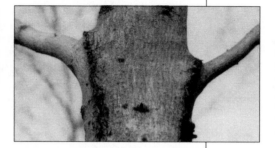

Figure 4-3. Directional pruning involves making a diagonal cut slightly above a bud in the area or direction in which you would like new growth to develop.

shears are not pruning shears and will not give the control needed to make correctly placed pruning cuts. Nor are hand shears large enough for removing larger branches (those with a diameter of 1 inch or more). When larger material must be removed, use loppers or a pruning saw, but for all jobs use equipment that makes a clean cut, which extends all the way through the plant part being removed without tearing the plant tissue in the process. Using the wrong equipment will damage the tree and could lead to its death.

SUCCESSFUL TRANSPLANTING

The two most critical factors in successfully moving trees and shrubs are to move the plants at the right time of year relative to their growth cycles, and to dig up and take as much of their root systems as possible.

Generally, the best time of year to move plants is while they are dormant. This time period may vary from several months between mid-fall and early spring in northern areas, to a month or so in late winter in the South. In the Deep South plants may never go into true dormancy, but may be more successfully moved when they are in a resting stage, a time when no new growth is being produced.

The best time to move most deciduous trees and shrubs is between the fall leaf-drop period and the time when buds break and active growth resumes again in spring. Root growth in the soil continues long after the above-ground portion of the plant has ceased growing, and generally does not stop until the temperature of the soil falls below 40°F. Frozen ground is the major obstacle to moving plants during the dormant period.

There are some exceptions to the above generalization. Certain species of trees and shrubs do not transplant or move as well in the fall and winter as they do in the spring when growth is resuming. Check with your local nursery or garden center or in a reference book about the particular plants you want to move, to see if any fit this category.

It is safe to assume that, once the deciduous plants have dropped their leaves, most evergreens are also fairly dormant. Their dormancy period is generally a bit shorter than that of deciduous plants, though. With a few exceptions, all evergreens should be moved before deciduous plants break bud.

Plants of all kinds can be moved at other times of the year if necessary. The key to successfully moving plants while they are actively growing is to minimize transplant stress by keeping them well watered and sheltered from the hot sun and drying winds until their roots have become reestablished.

The easiest plants to move and successfully replant are relatively small deciduous trees and shrubs. They can often be dug up and moved bare-rooted while they are dormant. At any other time, a ball of soil should be dug up with their roots.

With large trees and shrubs, and with all evergreens, a ball of soil that surrounds the roots should always be dug. Evergreens in particular should never be moved bare-rooted.

If you can anticipate far enough in advance which plants will be moved, it helps to "root prune" them at least several months prior to their move. Root pruning involves digging a narrow trench or breaking through the root system with a spade or shovel, outlining the root ball to be moved with the plant. This practice will help regenerate more roots within that root ball, so that a more extensive root system can be moved with the plant. Outline as large a root ball as possible, but remember that soil is heavy. For large and valuable plants, it may be necessary to have a piece of heavy equipment like a tree spade or a backhoe come in and dig up the plant.

Whether plants are dug bare-rooted or with a soil ball for moving, replant them as quickly as possible. Dig the planting holes at the new plant locations prior to digging up the plants to be moved, so that they can simply be taken from one location to the other and immediately replanted. Protect bare roots by wrapping them in a moist cloth or layers of moist newspaper.

When you dig a soil ball, slip a piece of burlap under and around the ball, to wrap the ball tight before moving it. Keep the soil ball moist — this will prevent it from falling apart. Dry soil should be watered before the soil ball is dug.

In addition to root pruning, pruning the top of the plant may be desirable prior to planting. Remove any broken or dying branches, do any corrective pruning that is needed, and, if size reduction is desired, prune the plant back in its natural form. Pruning prior to transplanting will reduce the moisture stress put on the leaves, but do not prune unless it is really needed.

To replant the items you are moving, follow the correct planting procedures outlined on pages 43-45.

SHOPPING FOR PLANTS BY MAIL

■ First and foremost, buy from reputable firms. Ask gardening friends which companies they purchase from, look for the Mailorder Association of Nurseries (MAN) logo in catalogs, or send for one of the prepared lists of mail-order sources that are often advertised in gardening magazines.

■ Read all catalog descriptions carefully. If the claims sound too fantastic or the prices seem too low, they probably are, and you'll get exactly what you pay for.

■ Be sure there is a guarantee policy, and check to see what you must keep to use it — a copy of your order or a cancelled check. It is always a good idea to keep a copy of your order for your records.

■ Have the items delivered to your place of employment if it is easier or if you order plants that could be damaged by being left out in the cold, wind, or heat. If you require a specific delivery date, be sure to state that.

■ When your order arrives, unpack it immediately and check to see that it is complete and that all the plants are labelled.

■ If items are missing, check for a statement explaining the omission (often it deals with plants being shipped according to their proper planting times). If no explanation is enclosed, contact the supplier immediately. If orders are damaged or plants are in poor condition, make immediate contact.

SHOPPING FOR PLANTS

When you are ready to buy new plants, buy good-quality specimens from reputable sources. It is possible to buy inexpensive plants, but be sure to distinguish between inexpensive and cheap ones. Mail-order nurseries can be a source for less expensive plants, but these plants will often be quite small, may get damaged during shipping, and may be inferior to what was pictured or claimed in the advertising.

■ Store all products as directed, and install plants as soon as possible. If planting must be delayed, either temporarily "heel plants in" (place them in a transitional outdoor bed), or check the roots for moisture, and moisten and repackage if necessary. Store plants to be held in a cool, dark location. If the plants are small, refrigerate them until planting is possible. If adequate planting directions have not been provided, request them.

SHOPPING FOR PLANTS IN PERSON

Look for these signs of healthy plants when buying plants in person at a nursery or from another supplier:

■ The plants should look healthy, with leaves of proper size and color, buds that are plump and firm, and adequate numbers of flowers and/or fruits on those that are specimen plants.

■ The plants should be free of insects and disease signs or symptoms (spotted leaves, cankers on twigs, etc.), and there should be no weeds growing in the pots.

■ Bare-rooted plants should have enough field roots, from which new roots (important for absorbing water and nutrients and anchoring the plant in the ground) will be able to regenerate.

■ The root balls of balled-and-burlapped plants should be adequate in size, and the wrapping material should be intact and firmly secured.

■ When the container is carefully pulled away from a container-grown or containerized plant to reveal the root ball, there should be white roots on the outside of the ball. If the plant has become root-bound, the roots will begin to circle around the outside of the root ball, and the possibility exists that the roots of the plant, particularly those of trees, could girdle or kill it.

■ The plants should have been carefully handled — no broken buds or branches and no scratched or damaged bark. The plants should be stored properly away from drying winds and scalding or freezing temperatures.

Be sure that you don't abuse the plants when you transport them and hold them at home prior to planting them. Shield them from wind and sun as much as possible while driving home, especially if they are evergreens or deciduous plants that have leafed out. Keep the soil balls of balled-and-burlapped, container-grown, processed-balled, and containerized plants evenly moist. Be sure not to drop balled-and-burlapped plants or carry them only by holding the trunks — you could break the root ball.

Finally, be sure to choose and locate trees and shrubs according to their appropriate environmental and growing needs. If a shrub that needs full sun is put in the shade, or a marginally hardy evergreen tree in the path of winter winds, the plant will be weakened by advrse growing conditions. Weakened plants are vulnerable to deadly insects and diseases.

PLANTING PROCEDURES

The first step in planting is to make sure the roots of the tree or shrub are thoroughly moistened. Soak bare-rooted specimens for an hour or two to rehydrate their roots. Water the soil of balled-and-burlapped or container-grown plants if it is dry.

In general, the planting hole should be dug to a diameter at least twice that of the root ball or root spread. For example, if the root ball has a 12-inch spread, dig a 24-inch diameter hole. The hole should be no deeper than the depth of the root system or root ball; digging the hole too deep can result in the root ball droppping below the planting level as the soil beneach the ball settles and compacts. This can lead to root suffocation or decay if water collects over and around the roots, or if soil washes in over the roots.

In heavy soils that drain poorly, it is often recommended that less than the total root ball be placed in the hole. Under these conditions a shallow hole can be dug, and the top of the ball that is exposed above ground covered with 2 or 3 inches of mulch for protection.

If the hole for a large tree or shrub is being dug with a tree spade, auger, or other piece of power equipment, and a planting hole with a glazed side results (common where the clay content is high), be sure to rough up the side prior to backfilling. A

Right

Wrong

Result

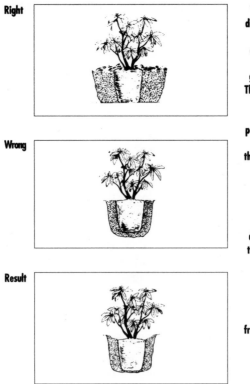

There is a proper way to dig a planting hole. When the planting hole is dug deeper than the root ball (center), settling will generally occur (bottom). This will leave the plant in a pit -- subject to root suffocation during wet periods or stem damage if soil or silt fills in around the stem. The proper way is to set a plant into a hole that is the same depth as the root ball; settling is then avoided and good root development will occur in the upper 10 to 12 inches of soil. In heavy soils (which do not always drain well), you may leave a small portion of the root ball protruding from the soil; protect that small protrusion with a layer of mulch (top).

glazed planting hole can act like an in-ground container and keep the roots from penetrating into the surrounding soil.

If the tree or shrub is bare-rooted, prune off any broken, damaged, or diseased roots, then hold the plant in place while you begin to backfill. Hold the plant so that the soil level will be at the same level as it was in the field. There will generally be a color difference on the stem that will indicate this level.

If the plant is balled-and-burlapped, place the ball in the hole and either cut it several times or remove the wrapping material if it is not cotton burlap. Even if biodegradable wrapping material is used, roots will grow out more quickly if the wrapping material is cut or partially removed (at least be sure that it does not sit exposed on the surface, where it can quickly dry out). Remove any nails or pins used to hold the ball together, and especially any rope or twine tied around the ball and/or trunk. If the ball of a large tree or shrub was placed in a wire basket after the ball was wrapped, remove the wire basket prior to placing the root ball in the hole, or clip the basket apart if it is to remain in the hole. Wire baskets do not decay as rapidly as organic materials and can cause serious root deformation.

If a field-grown tree or shrub has been dug with a soil ball and placed in a fiber pot, the pot can be planted as long as you remove any margin of the pot that protrudes above the ground. Fiber pots can be removed if the roots haven't begun to grow into them too extensively, but if you meet much resistance in trying to remove the pot, leave it on to avoid possible root damage.

The major reason for digging a wide planting hole is to have plenty of soil that can be "fluffed up" or aerated for backfilling around the root system or ball. Where once a variety of organic additions, most notably peat moss, were recommended for incorporation into the backfill soil at some percentage, this is no longer the recommended practice, regardless of the soil or plant type (not even for acid-loving plants such as azaleas). It has been discovered that any addition to the backfill soil can hamper growth and even kill the plant.

Backfill the planting hole approximately one-half to two-thirds full, tamp the soil down firmly, then water the soil well and wait until all of the water has drained through before backfilling the remainder of the hole. This will insure that the backfill soil will be moist and won't dry out the roots by absorbing water from them; it will also help to settle out any major air pockets. If the soil is particularly wet when you want to plant, try to wait until it has dried somewhat before digging your hole. Working wet soil can ruin its structure and compact it, causing it to drain poorly, cake over, and shed water.

Organic fertilizers and slow-release inorganic fertilizers (often in compressed or pellet form) should be incorporated at backfill time. Be sure to follow the recommended dosage, and be sure not to use a fast-release inorganic fertilizer that could absorb water from the roots, causing them to "burn."

Wrapping, Staking, Mulching, Pruning

Consider wrapping the trunks of thin-barked trees that have been planted in late spring or summer, because the bark could be damaged by high temperatures or excess water loss.

45

Always start wrapping from the soil line upward to just beneath the lowest branch, so that water will be shed down the wrapping and not funneled in beneath it where it can cause the bark to decay. Wrap in overlapping spirals that will put two thicknesses

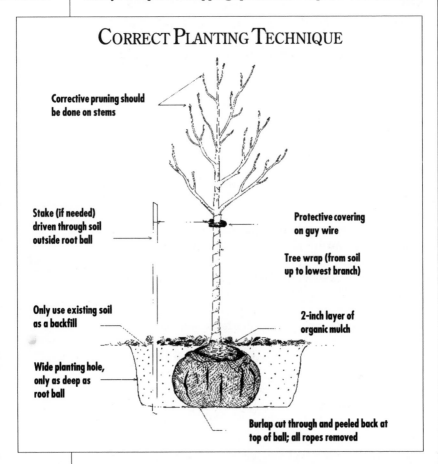

CORRECT PLANTING TECHNIQUE

Corrective pruning should
be done on stems

Stake (if needed)
driven through soil
outside root ball

Protective covering
on guy wire

Tree wrap (from soil
up to lowest branch)

Only use existing soil
as a backfill

2-inch layer of
organic mulch

Wide planting hole,
only as deep as
root ball

Burlap cut through and peeled back at
top of ball; all ropes removed

of wrapping around the trunk. Whenever possible, use a biodegradable material such as burlap or a special tree-wrap paper, and always remove the tree wrap within a year or two of planting.

Trees should be staked only if they are in an exposed area where they may physically blow over in their planting hole, or if their crowns are disproportionately large for their root balls. Trees that do not need to be staked shouldn't be; unstaked trees develop stronger and more flexible stems because they are allowed to move with the wind. They also tend to develop stems of larger caliper (diameter) than their staked counterparts.

When staking, or "guying," trees you can choose from a variety of staking methods and products. Select one that minimizes damage to the roots or trunk and, where possible, leave the tree an inch or two of space in which to flex. If stakes will be

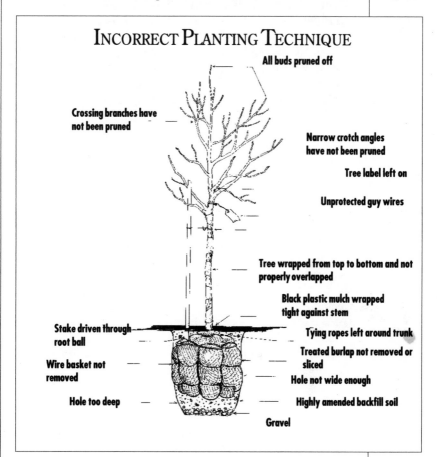

INCORRECT PLANTING TECHNIQUE

All buds pruned off

Crossing branches have not been pruned

Narrow crotch angles have not been pruned

Tree label left on

Unprotected guy wires

Tree wrapped from top to bottom and not properly overlapped

Black plastic mulch wrapped tight against stem

Stake driven through root ball

Tying ropes left around trunk

Wire basket not removed

Treated burlap not removed or sliced

Hole not wide enough

Hole too deep

Highly amended backfill soil

Gravel

positioned in the planting hole, install them prior to backfilling the soil, so that you can avoid driving them into any roots.

Cover any twine, rope, or wire that is wrapped around the trunk with a protective material, and remove all guying and staking materials after one year.

All trees and shrubs should be mulched after planting. Mulching serves not only to help conserve soil moisture and keep grass and weed growth down, but it also keeps the soil temperature cooler in the summer and warmer in the winter, thus extending the time during which root growth will be active. Another important function of mulch is to keep lawn mowers,

47

string trimmers, and other equipment from running into or damaging the trunk or bark.

Use 2 to 3 inches of an organic mulch, such as peat moss, shredded or chunk pine bark, rotted sawdust, compost, or pine needles. A mulch deeper than 2 to 3 inches can encourage overly shallow root development, can become waterlogged, and can encourage bark decay and foraging by rodents, especially if piled directly against the tree trunk. Do not use black plastic or any type of pebbles or rocks to mulch trees or shrubs.

Mulches should be used for at least the first few years around newly transplanted trees and shrubs while their roots are reestablishing. Their continued use around plants after that will help to minimize equipment damage to the plants.

Maintaining Healthy Trees and Shrubs

Watering

The main reason that newly planted trees and shrubs die is because no one continues to water them once they've been planted. Watering them at planting time and then never again is simply not sufficient.

Trees and shrubs should be watered regularly for at least the first year or two after planting whenever there is insufficient rainfall. Check local references to see how much rain your area receives on a weekly basis. In most areas (with modifications for soil type or exposure), at least 1 to 1½ inches of water per week, from a combination of rain and supplemental watering, should be available to your landscape plants during the active growing season.

Be sure to adopt good water management practices, such as applying water long enough to saturate the soil to a depth of at least 6 to 8 inches (and preferably to 1 foot or more) to encourage deep rooting of plants. Try to use irrigation equipment that keeps the water on or as close to the soil surface as possible to decrease the wasteful evaporation of water applied overhead.

Fertilizing

If you are applying a lawn grass fertilizer regularly, it will also be feeding the root systems of any trees or shrubs in the same area. The rates recommended for lawn fertilization are generally high enough to feed both the lawn and the landscape plants, although it is always a good idea to have a soil test run prior to applying fertilizer to be sure what nutrients are needed.

Full-page photo: **Assorted crocuses.** MADELAINE GRAY. **Inset:** A mass planting of red tulips. MADELAINE GRAY. **Previous page:** An azalea garden. ANN REILLY: PHOTO/NATS.

Full-page photo: Hydrangea and rose blossoms.
MARGARITE BRADLEY/POSITIVE IMAGES. **Inset: Lilac blossoms.** JOHN A. LYNCH: PHOTO/NATS.

Full-page photo: Roses growing on a fence. JERRY HOWARD/POSITIVE IMAGES. **Inset: A flowering forsythia shrub (*Forsythia* x *intermedia*).** ROBERT E. LYONS: PHOTO/NATS.

Full-page photo: A tall-growing rhododendron.
DAVID M. STONE: PHOTO/NATS. **Inset, top: Japanese barberry (*Berberis thunbergii* 'Crimson Pygmy').**
ROBERT E. LYONS: PHOTO/NATS. **Inset, above: Juniper shrubs used as a border.** ROBERT E. LYONS: PHOTO/NATS.

A soil test is also important so that a desirable pH (level of soil acidity) can be maintained (see pages 23-24).

Supplemental fertilizer may need to be applied where a lawn is not fed or where there is no lawn to feed. In addition, trees, shrubs, and perennials in separate beds that do not receive any peripheral lawn fertilizer will also need feeding.

A major misconception regarding plant growth is that tree and shrub roots stop at the drip line (directly under the plant's canopy). This is far from true, since plant roots, especially those of trees, can extend great distances beyond their drip lines. In particular, the small fibrous roots that absorb the bulk of a tree's water and nutrients are those that grow a considerable distance beyond it.

Fertilization is also important for landscape plants that have been damaged physically or by a pest organism. Keeping plants strong and healthy will minimize the ability of pest organisms to attack plants, and will help promote the healing process. Whenever you do fertilize, however, be sure that adequate water is available for nutrient uptake. Never fertilize under drought conditions or when water cannot be applied; damaged plants should be fertilized at a reduced rate (generally half the normal rate). A good time to apply fertilizer is when rain is forecast.

Insect and Pest Control

A two-sided approach should be developed for all disease and insect problems once they've been correctly identified. First, how do you control or correct the problem right now, and second, how do you control, or preferably prevent the problem in the future? Often a chemical will kill all the targeted insect pests immediately, but it may also kill beneficial insects, which are desirable to have because they feed on or parasitize those same pest insects.

Wherever possible, remove plants that have major pest problems and replace them with varieties or cultivars of the same plant that are more pest-resistant or -tolerant. Or avoid the problem altogether and just do not use that plant in your landscape again. When you shop for new plants, find out what potential pest problems they have and whether those problems are hard to control. In many cases it will be better to simply avoid problem trees and shrubs altogether.

When pest problems do occur in your landscape, try to remove any damaged plant parts as quickly as possible. Sanitation and cleanup are very important. If you remove the diseased leaves or twigs that can harbor an insect over the winter, then the organism will not reinfect or reinfest your plants the following season.

If you have one diseased plant in the midst of several healthy plants, get rid of it before the problem spreads to other plants. This is easy if it means just pulling out one small flowering plant or shrub, but can be difficult if it means removing a large tree. A serious problem in controlling tree diseases is the fact that tree roots will graft together underground and a disease organism can spread from tree to tree by way of the grafted root systems.

Some pest problems are soil-borne (inhabit the soil). On a small scale, it may sometimes be possible to dig out infested or infected soil and replace it with "clean" topsoil. But where this measure is impractical, there are ways, with chemicals and solar heat, to sterilize the soil and kill off the pest organisms, often without damaging desirable organisms.

Chapter 5
15 Favorite Trees and Shrubs

Among the advantages of trees and shrubs are that they live longer and require less care than perennial flowers or bedding plants. Plant a shrub once and you'll enjoy it for a lifetime. Most trees and shrubs have large and efficient root systems, which give them a survival edge. They rarely need extra water and thrive in all different types of soil and weather conditions.

Hardy shrubs and trees are hard to kill. They are tough enough to take cold winds, long winters, and early frosts. Insects and disease ignore most hardy trees and shrubs. These plant enemies prefer to attack the soft and succulent growth of tender annual flowers and perennials. Trees and shrubs can also be used to solve problems. They can hold the soil on a steep hillside, screen an ugly view, block the wind, and define your garden boundaries.

With all these advantages, it's no wonder that landscape planners, whether professional or amateur, rely on trees and shrubs to add color and visual interest with a minimum of care.

In the remainder of this chapter, we'll describe 15 favorite trees and shrubs. The term shrub, by the way, is not a scientific one. It generally denotes any multi-trunked woody perennial plant whose mature height is shorter than a tree.

For each type of shrub or tree described, you'll find an indication of the most northerly zone in which the particular type will survive the winter. The zone map is on page 63. Remember as you choose trees and shrubs to pick them based not only on your general geographical zone, but also on the specific location where they will live — sunny or shady, wet or dry, northern or southern exposure, etc. — in your landscape.

Finally, the trees and shrubs described here by no means exhaust the possibilities. They were chosen because they are among the most popular. A comprehensive gardening encyclopedia will offer many more possibilities.

Azalea (Genus: Rhododendron)

The various shrubs commonly known as azaleas are all members of the *Rhododendron* genus, which has two basic types of plants: deciduous and evergreen. Azaleas described

51

here are all deciduous; for evergreen azaleas, see Rhododendron on page 58.

Azaleas grow well in either full sun or partial shade and prefer moist, acid soil. If your soil is not naturally acidic, there are both natural and chemical products available at garden centers to increase its acidity. Most azaleas are hardy to Zone 5 or Zone 6.

AZALEA

The majority of azaleas bloom in early spring, although two bloom later than other varieties (*R. arborescens* and *R. calendulaceum*). Blossoms vary in size from slightly more than 1 inch across (*R. atlanticum*) to 3 inches (Knap Hill hybrids), with several varieties having 2-inch flowers. Flower colors include pink, rose, yellow, salmon, orange, scarlet, and white, depending on the variety chosen. The blooms of two varieties are fragrant (*R. albrechtii* and *R. atlanticum*).

Leaves of the *R. schlippenbachii* and *R. arborescens* strains turn red in the fall, while the foliage of Knap Hill hybrids turns either red or yellow.

The mature heights of azaleas vary considerably. *R. atlanticum*, also known as Coast or Dwarf, reaches a mature height of only 2 feet. *R. schlippenbachii*, on the other hand, is a tall slender plant, reaching a mature height of 15 feet. Several strains have mature heights of 5 feet (*R. albrechtii,* Knap Hill hybrids, and *R. molle*, also known as Chinese azalea).

Azaleas are often used in beds, as foundation plantings, as accents and, space permitting, in mass plantings.

Barberry (Genus: Berberis)

Small yellow flowers in the spring followed by red berries that birds love to eat characterize the cheerful barberry.

Barberries are easily sheared to keep them in shape, which is why they are often recommended for low to mid-height hedges, screens, or barrier plantings. They are also effective as specimen plants.

Barberries have thorny twigs, which means they are not generally suitable for locations (for example, near walkways) where they will be in close contact with people.

Barberries grow well either in full sun or partial shade and are tolerant of most types of soil. Depending on the variety chosen, they are hardy in zones 5 through 7. The Mentor barberry (*B.* x *mentorensis*) is an evergreen in zones 6 through 10; it is also more heat- and drought-resistant than the other varieties.

Flower size varies from ¼ to ½ inch. The yellow flowers of one variety (*B. thunbergii*, or Japanese barberry) are bordered with red. Foliage is generally green, although there are varieties of the Japanese barberry with red leaves.

Mature heights vary from 2 feet (dwarf form of *B. thunbergii*) to 5 feet (regular *B. thunbergii*).

DOGWOOD (GENUS: CORNUS)

For sheer magnificence, few sights can match a blooming dogwood in the spring. The lovely dogwood is also one of the best bets for visual interest throughout the year. Following the blooms, berries appear, which are relished by the birds. Dogwood leaves turn red or reddish green in the fall.

Dogwoods need either full sun or partial shade. They are tolerant of most soil types. Their uses in the landscape include hedges, screens, or specimen plants.

The Cornelian cherry (*C. mas*) has small yellow flowers in 1-inch clusters. Other varieties have white blossoms, varying in size from 1 to 3 inches. The flowers of the Japanese dogwood (*C. kousa*) gradually turn pinkish.

The berries that follow the flowers vary from red (Cornelian and Japanese) to white (*C. sericea*, or Red-osier) to bluish white (*C. alba*, or Tartarian dogwood); there is also a variety of Cornelian cherry called 'Flava' that has yellow berries.

Blooming time varies from early spring (Cornelian cherry) to late spring (Japanese and Tartarian) to late spring through midsummer (Red-osier).

Cornelian cherry and Japanese dogwood are hearty to Zone 5. Those species that can survive colder climates include Red-osier and Tartarian (both Zone 2). These cool-zone dogwoods have vivid red or yellow twigs in the winter, which makes them much prized for providing winter color in the landscape. They thrive particularly in moist areas, such as on the banks of ponds or streams.

Dogwoods are tall shrubs, although there may be some dwarf specimens available. Heights of most varieties range between 10 and 20 feet.

FORSYTHIA (GENUS: FORSYTHIA)

Forsythias massed with golden blossoms are one of the

first signs in many landscapes that winter is surely over. Hardy and vigorous, forsythias need plenty of space to grow; be sure not to plant them too close to other plants. Once their early-spring blossoms have faded, forsythias put forth dark green leaves. The thick green bushes make excellent barriers and screens and superb specimen plants in the early spring, although they lack the year-round seasonal interest of some other types of shrubs. Forsythias are tolerant of most soil types and thrive in either full sun or partial shade.

Three varieties of forsythias are generally available. All are hardy to Zone 5.

The 'Arnold Dwarf' forsythia hybrid is a low-growing variety (4 feet in height) with arching branches that root on contact with the ground, producing a dense foliage mat. It is especially prized for use as a groundcover and on slopes to stabilize soil. Its blossoms are small and greenish yellow in color.

There are many varieties of the Border forsythia (*F.* x *intermedia*), such as 'Spring Glory' and 'Spectabilis'. This plant reaches a height of 10 feet. Its blooms are about 2 inches long and a yellow-gold color. It should be pruned after it finishes flowering.

The Korean golden bell, or early forsythia (*F. ovata*), is the most cold-hardy of the forsythias and the earliest bloomer. It reaches a height of 5 feet. Flowers measure 1 to 1½ inches and are yellow-gold.

HYDRANGEA (GENUS: HYDRANGEA)

For its long-lasting and showy color display all through midsummer, the hydrangea has earned its place as a favorite shrub.

The individual flowers of hydrangeas are actually quite small. The blossoms are born in clusters measuring anywhere from 6 to 12 inches, depending on the variety. These clusters, when viewed at a distance, give the impression of huge flower balls.

Hydrangeas thrive in full sun or partial shade. They need moist, well-drained, and rich soil.

The flowers of Hills-of-Snow (*H. arborescens* 'Grandiflora') and Oak-leaved (*H. quercifolia*) hydrangeas are white; their flower clusters measure about 6 inches across. The foot-long clusters of Peegee hydrangea (*H. paniculata* 'Grandiflora') flowers start out white, then gradually turn to pink or purple. The dried flowers cling to the plant through much of the winter, and can be brought inside for dried flower arrangements.

The 5- to 10-inch rounded clusters of French hydrangea (*H. macrophylla*) flowers may be either white, blue, or pink, depending on soil pH. Acid soil produces pink flowers; alkaline soil produces blue flowers; and neutral soil produces white flowers. This is the type of hydrangea frequently sold as a houseplant in the spring; after blooming inside the house it can then be transplanted outdoors.

Hills-of-Snow and Peegee hydrangeas are hardy to Zone 4. The French variety is hardy to Zone 5 or 6. Oak-leaved hydrangeas are hardy to Zone 5. The Oak-leaved species produces red leaves in the fall.

Mature heights of hydrangeas range from 30 feet for the Peegee (which can be trained to tree form), to 5 to 8 feet for the French, 6 feet for the Oak-leaved, and 4 feet for Hills-of-Snow.

The French and Hills-of-Snow hydrangeas die back in winter in colder areas.

Hills-of-Snow should be pruned in early spring before new growth begins. The French and Oak-leaved species should be pruned after they flower. Pruning encourages the Peegee hydrangea to grow larger.

The French and Hills-of-Snow hydrangeas make good foundation plantings or shrub borders. Because it spreads so much, the Oak-leaved hydrangea is best planted alone, as is the Peegee because it grows so large.

JUNIPER (GENUS: JUNIPERUS)

Of all the coniferous shrubs, juniper is one of the most popular for foundation plantings — and with good reason. Junipers with mature heights below 4 feet (including several with maximum heights of only 1 to 2 feet), are just the right height to hide foundations without overpowering a house. Their dense growing habit ideally suits them to hide foundations, and the low-growing junipers can be pruned at any time.

All the junipers except the Shore juniper (*J. conferta*) are hardy to Zone 3 or 4, which means they can be grown virtually anywhere in the United States. The Shore juniper prefers sandy seashore locations and is ideal as a groundcover in sandy, hard-to-plant areas. It is hardy to Zone 6.

A juniper that is ideal for a groundcover in non-sandy locations and well suited to sloping areas is the Creeping juniper (*J. horizontalis*), which has a maximum height of 1 foot. It has either blue-green or steel-blue needles and is covered with handsome blue berries in the fall. Its color actually intensifies in the winter.

Only two junipers grow taller than 4 feet. One is the Pfitzer (*J. chinensis* 'Pfitzeriana'). This fast-growing, flat-topped variety is the only juniper that tolerates partial shade. It reaches 6 feet in height. To keep its shape, it needs constant pruning, but it is often attractive in foundation plantings when used with other plants.

The other taller juniper is the Hollywood (*J. chinensis* 'Torulosa'), which reaches a mature height of 20 feet. It is used as a specimen tree by those who like its interesting, twisted branching habit.

LILAC (GENUS: SYRINGA)

For a few magic weeks in late spring, those who have lilacs enjoy the pleasant sensation of perfumed air. No flowering shrub produces such intensely fragrant blossoms as the lilac.

LILAC

Lilacs need well-drained soil and a sunny location. They leaf early and drop their leaves late. They do best where winters are cold. Mature heights range from 6 to 20 feet.

To promote more blossoms and better growth the following year, remove dying flowers and seed clusters after the flowers fade. Young, unwanted suckers should also be removed, but some should be left to promote plant vigor. Old wood should be pruned out when the plant is dormant.

In addition to the namesake color lilac, the flowers of lilacs may be red-purple, blue, pink, white, yellow, or red-violet, depending on the variety chosen. Lilac flowers are borne in clusters from 4 to 8 inches long, depending on the variety.

Lilacs make superb specimen plants. They are also used as hedges, screens, and windbreaks.

Lilac hardiness varies with the species. It ranges from Zone 6 (Meyer's, *S. meyeri*) to especially cold-resistant varieties that are hardy to Zone 2 — Late (*S. villosa*) and Preston (*S.* x *prestoniae*).

The Common lilac (*S. vulgaris*) is the most widely grown type. It is hardy to Zone 4 and highly cold-resistant. There are over 400 varieties in a full range of colors. Flower clusters are 6 to 8 inches long.

For later blooms, choose the Hungarian lilac (*S. josikaea*), which has reddish purple flowers, or the Late lilac, which has rose or white flowers and a fragrance different from other species. If you prefer a smaller lilac, choose Persian (*S. x persica*), which bears either violet or white flowers. For large, dense plants to be used as a screen or windbreak, try the Preston lilac; the flowers of this hybrid are less fragrant than those of other lilacs. For a hedge, Littleleaf (*S. microphylla*) is often used because it grows broadly, often twice as wide as it is high; it reaches a mature height of 6 to 8 feet. Flowers are reddish violet or pink.

MAGNOLIA (GENUS: MAGNOLIA)

If you live in Zone 6 or a warmer zone, you may wish to plant what many consider to be one of the most magnificent of trees: the magnolia. There are two types of trees commonly known as magnolias, each with its own unique qualities.

The tree that most readily comes to mind when most people think of magnolias is the Southern magnolia (*M. grandiflora*). This evergreen has broad, flat leaves that are replaced every two years. The Southern magnolia needs plenty of growing room, as it reaches a mature size of 90 feet tall and 80 feet wide, providing medium to dense shade. It needs moist, well-drained soil and is hardy to Zone 7. This tree is adorned with 8-inch creamy-white flowers from spring through midsummer.

The Saucer magnolia (*M. x soulangiana*) is deciduous. In early spring, before its leaves appear, it is covered with 5- to 10-inch, white-purple, cup-shaped flowers. Its bark is an attractive slate gray color. Leaves turn brown in the fall. It requires moist, well-drained soil. At maturity it can reach 25 feet in height and width. It provides light shade and is hardy to Zone 6.

MOCK ORANGE (GENUS: PHILADELPHUS)

For white 1- to 2-inch, single or double blooms in early summer, a mock orange is your best choice.

Mock oranges are hardy to Zone 5. They grow well in full sun or partial shade. An advantage for gardeners with little time is that mock oranges seldom need any pruning, except of deadwood. They are used primarily in shrub borders or as specimen plants.

The blossoms of the Sweet (*P. coronarius*) and 'Virginal' (*P. x virginalis*) mock oranges are very fragrant. The Sweet mock orange is tolerant of most soil types; it is also more tolerant of dry conditions than most other shrubs. Virginal and Lemoine (*P. x lemoinei*) hybrids need rich, well-drained soil.

The foliage of Sweet mock oranges turns yellow in the fall. Heights vary from 4 to 8 feet (Lemoine), to 10 feet (Sweet), to 5 to 9 feet (Virginal). A dwarf version of the Virginal mock orange stands about 3 feet tall.

MOUNTAIN-LAUREL (KALMIA LATIFOLIA)

Mountain-laurel is one answer to the question, "What shrub can I plant in a partially shady spot?"

This hardy (to Zone 5), broad-leafed evergreen likes moist, acid soil. It usually does not need much pruning; when it does, pruning should be done after flowers fade. It is most often used in shrub borders or in mass plantings. Mature height is 10 feet.

Small flowers, in 3- to 6-inch clusters, appear in early summer. Colors include white, pink, and rose. The 'Fuscata' variety has a purple band on the inside of each flower. After the flowers fade, cut off the developing seed capsules to promote more vigorous growth.

PRIVET (GENUS: LIGUSTRUM)

Privet is a hardy, pest-resistant evergreen shrub for screens, hedges, and shrub borders — ideal if you live in Zone 7 or warmer. It grows well in full sun or partial shade and tolerates most soil types. It can be pruned both after new growth appears and later in the season.

Chinese privet (*L. sinense*) produces 2- to 4-inch flower clusters in midsummer. Its foliage is glossy green. It is hardy to Zone 7 and reaches a height of 12 feet.

Glossy privet (*L. lucidum*) grows to 30 feet and it is hardy to Zone 8. Its flowers appear in 4- to 8-inch clusters in late summer and are followed by blue-black berries. There is a tri-color variety with pale yellow leaf margins that have a pinkish tone when young.

Japanese privet (*L. japonicum*) flowers in 3- to 6-inch clusters in midsummer, followed occasionally by blue-black berries. Its foliage is dark green above and light green below.

RHODODENDRON (GENUS: RHODODENDRON)

Evergreen rhododendrons are low-growing, dense, spreading shrubs often used in beds, foundation plantings, shrub borders, rock gardens, or in mass plantings for a showy and colorful display. They thrive in partial shade and well-drained, acid soil. They perform better if they are kept mulched. Fading flowers should be removed to promote more vigorous flowering the next year. Rhododendrons all have glossy green foliage.

The most popular rhododendrons are the Glenn Dale hybrids. There are more than 400 varieties with a wide range of blossom colors. Glenn Dales bloom in spring, bearing 1- to 3-inch single or double flowers. They reach a mature height of 5 feet. Most varieties are hardy to Zone 7, though a few can be successfully grown as far north as Zone 5.

The Kaempferi hybrids (*R.* x *Kaempferi*), of which numerous varieties are available, are spring bloomers with a range of blossom colors displayed in their 2- to 3-inch single flowers. They reach a height of 6 feet and are hardy to Zone 7.

For early summer flowering, choose Indica (*R. indicum*). Colors of the 2- to 4-inch flower clusters range through many shades of pink and violet.

If a more low-growing rhododendron is needed, there are the Kurume hybrids, whose mature height is only 3 feet. Another spring bloomer, it produces ½- to 1-inch single or double flowers in clusters of two to four. There are about 50 varieties available, most hardy to Zone 7.

ROSE-OF-SHARON (HIBISCUS SYRIACUS)

The shrub popularly known as Rose-of-Sharon is actually a hibiscus. It is sold both under these two names and under the name althea. This shrub is often used in narrow, hard-to-plant areas. It is useful for hedges or screens and is also an attractive specimen plant.

Rose-of-Sharon is valued especially for its late summer bloom, when few other shrubs are in bloom. Colors of the 2- to 4-inch single, double, or semi-double flowers include white, pink, red, blue, and violet bicolors, depending on the variety grown.

Rose-of-Sharon needs moist, well-drained soil and full sun or partial shade. It is hardy to Zone 5 and in seashore locations. Young plants must have winter protection in cold areas.

This shrub can be trained to tree form. It reaches a mature height of 6 to 10 feet or more.

ROSES (GENUS: ROSA)

Entire books are devoted to the growing of roses. Here we will only talk about some of the important information you'll need to decide whether roses should be part of your landscape, and about the many types that are available.

Roses must have well-drained soil. Most varieties also

require at least six full hours of sun a day. They do best when they get most of their sun in the morning and light shade in the afternoon. They prefer a slightly acid soil — 6.0 to 6.5 pH. Usually, hybrid teas, grandifloras, or floribundas should be spaced about 2 feet apart for good air circulation. Shrub and old garden roses should be spaced from 4 to 6 feet apart, depending on their size. They should be planted where their roots will not compete with roots from other trees or shrubs.

ROSES

Roses vary in their ability to survive cold winters. Hybrid teas, grandifloras, and floribundas need protection wherever temperatures fall below 20°F. One way to provide it is by covering the canes with a mound of soil at least 20 inches high. Remove the winter protection before new growth starts in the spring. For those who live in cold climates, there are now roses especially bred to survive colder winters.

Although some types of roses deserve the reputation of being a plant that needs an awful lot of TLC from a devoted gardener, not all types are so fussy. Shrub roses, for example, tolerate a good deal of neglect and a variety of growing conditions. They vary in height, from groundcovers to tall screens. Shrub roses have single or semi-double flowers that appear in the spring. Colors include pink, red, yellow, and copper.

Moyesi and rugosa are two popular tall-growing hybrid shrub roses that are hardy, disease-resistant, and not very demanding. They blossom all summer. Rugosa does well in seaside locations.

Climbing roses will grow on any type of support, with a little training. They will also grow across the top of a fence. The most vigorous growers of the climbing roses are called ramblers.

Tree roses, also called "standards," have trunks as tall as 3 feet. They are useful as accents in a flower bed or near an entrance or patio. Their trunks must be supported by stakes and wrapped in burlap while young, because the bark is sensitive to light. To survive, they must also be heavily protected in the winter.

Hybrid teas, floribundas, and grandifloras are the three types of modern roses.

Hybrid teas have pointed buds, high-centered blooms, and long stems, which makes them perfect as cut flowers. There are many colors and color combinations. They are generally hardy to Zone 5. They bloom intermittently throughout the summer, usually giving their most impressive displays in early and late summer.

Floribundas produce clusters of flowers all through the summer. Many experts believe they make the most impressive display when several of one kind and color are planted together. Floribunda blooms may be either single or double. They are quite attractive, but they do not have as long a stem or as perfect a form as hybrid tea blossoms. They are valued more for show and duration than for their single blooms.

Grandiflora is the newest class of rose and represents a cross between hybrid teas and floribundas. It has longer cutting stems than the floribundas and blooms more prolifically than the hybrid teas. Grandifloras have taller bushes than most floribundas.

Hybrid teas, floribundas, and grandifloras require attention to keep them free of insects and diseases. Frequent inspection is needed to catch pests at the first sign of trouble. It is a good idea to plan beds for these types of roses close to your regular entrances or exits from your home. That way, you can regularly stop by the rose bed to look over the bushes.

SPIREA (GENUS: SPIRAEA)

Whether you're looking for a shrub that blooms in spring, summer, or fall, a spirea could be the answer. There are varieties of spirea that bloom at the desired time. Spireas thrive in full sun or partial shade and tolerate most soil types. Characteristics of each type are outlined in the table below.

NAME	ZONE	DESCRIPTION	HEIGHT	COMMENTS
Big Nippon (S. nipponica rotundifolia)	5	Blue-green foliage. Tiny white flowers in clusters in early spring.	5'-8'	Has more upright growth than other spireas. Good for shrub borders and specimen plant. Prune after flowers fade.
Billiard (S. x billiardii)	5	Very small pink-red flowers in 8" pyramid-shaped cones. Blooms midsummer through fall.	6'	Shrub borders or mass plantings. Reproduces quickly by underground stolons to form dense mass. Prune in early spring while dormant.

Name	Zone	Description	Height	Comments
Bridalwreath (S. prunifolia)	5	½", double white flowers line branches in mid-spring. Leaves turn red-orange in fall.	6'	Long, showy, arching branches. Prune after flowers fade.
Bumalda (S. x bumalda)	6	Tiny pink flowers in 4"-6" spike-shaped clusters appear in midsummer and often last through fall.	2'	Trimming old flowers prolongs blooming. Prune in early spring while dormant. Froebeli variety grows slightly taller.
Garland (S. x arguta)	5	Tiny white flowers in small flat, clusters cover the branches in spring.	3'-6'	Showy, arching branches. Dwarf variety is good for foundation plantings. Prune after flowers fade.
Japanese, Mikado (S. 'Atrosanguinea')	6	Tiny red flowers in 2"-5" flat clusters in early summer.	6'	Low-growing form can be used in rock japonica gardens and edgings. Prune in early spring while dormant.
Reeve's (S. cantoniensis)	7	Tiny white flowers in 1"-2" clusters in late spring. Leaves turn red-brown in fall.	5'	Showy, arching branches. Semi-evergreen in warm areas. Prune after flowers fade.
Thunberg (S. thunbergii)	5	½" flowers in clusters of 2-5 appear in mid-spring. Leaves turn yellow in fall.	5'	Very showy. Blooms earlier than most others. Often loses some branches in cold winters, so pruning is needed to keep plant neat. Prune after flowers fade.
Vanhoutte (S. x vanhouttei)	4	½" white flowers in 1"-2" clusters in late spring. Leaves turn red-orange in fall.	5'	Most widely grown spirea. Very showy and hardy. Prune after flowers fade.

Planting Zone Map

Approximate Range of Average Annual Mimimum Temperature for Each Zone

ZONE 1	BELOW -50°F
ZONE 2	-50° TO -40°
ZONE 3	-40° TO -30°
ZONE 4	-30° TO -20°
ZONE 5	-20° TO -10°
ZONE 6	-10° TO 0°
ZONE 7	0° TO 10°
ZONE 8	10° TO 20°
ZONE 9	20° TO 30°
ZONE 10	30° TO 40°

Chapter 6

Landscaping with Bulbs

Spring Bulbs in the Landscape

What says SPRING better than a magnificent bulb display, especially when it is tastefully integrated into the rest of the landscape? Long before any other plant contributes color to the garden, bulbs such as winter aconite, snowdrops, bulbous iris, early-blooming species crocus, and later-blooming hybrid crocus are poking their heads through the ground, leaves, and even snow.

A little later, Grecian windflower, Siberian squill, and glory-of-the-snow show off their blooms, when days are still bleak and trees and shrubs are just beginning to think about blossoming or leafing out. All of these early bulbs can be naturalized in the lawn, as it has not yet started to grow.

In front of forsythia, early tulips and daffodils form an enchanting silhouette, united by a border of pansies. Fragrant hyacinths bloom at the same time as most daffodils and can be added to this scheme, under magnolias or in front of rhododendrons. Grape hyacinths, blooming a little later, add complementary blue to the pinks of flowering crabapple, cherry, and peach trees. With late-blooming azaleas and dogwood, combine Dutch iris and wood hyacinth. Allium can add color and accent to early perennials, such as irises and peonies.

Late-blooming tulips, hyacinths, and daffodils bloom with shrubs and early perennials and should become a part of your overall landscape plan. Being larger, they can deliver a greater impact and help to fill the time voids between early bulbs, flowering trees and shrubs, and summer annuals.

Set early-blooming bulbs where you and passers-by will notice them the most. Besides growing in the lawn, they do well around the base of trees near the house, or in small clumps near the front door. Line the path to the door or from the garage to the house. Squeeze them into the corner of the rock garden or use them as a border in front of the foundation planting. Pick complementary heights and colors and select different types, so color will be continuous and even overlap.

Tulips and hyacinths are most effective when planted in masses in the flower bed or border. After their flowers fade, color can be achieved with perennials or annuals. If you grow roses, interplant daffodils between the rose plants and line the beds with crocuses. The result will be color for many months before the roses bloom.

Many bulbs like full sun, but since most spring bulbs bloom before the trees leaf out, they will be in the sun anyway. You will find that those bulbs planted in a shaded spot will bloom a little later, will have a more intense color, and will last somewhat longer.

PLANNING THE BULB PLANTING

The first decision to make in planning a bulb planting is whether you want a formal or informal look for the garden. The style of your home and the rest of the garden may determine this for you. The formal garden, as the name implies, is a more symmetrical garden with regular borders; it should be planted with formal bulbs such as tulips and hyacinths and should use blocks of one or two colors. Informal beds are more natural in appearance, with bulbs planted in natural-looking drifts and in a rainbow of colors.

When choosing bulbs for the garden design, select a number of types, so that you will have color from late winter until early summer. By ensuring a *succession of bloom*, you ensure continuous color.

Almost without exception, bulbs look better when planted in *clumps of at least three.* The smaller the bulb, the more flowers you need in the clump. For example, plant four clumps, with three tulips in each clump, across a 9-foot section of the foundation planting, rather than planting the tulips single file, 9 inches apart, in an empty-looking line.

Formal or informal, bulb plantings look best when individual clumps do not contain more than one color and sometimes not more than one variety. When you plan out your design, figure on enough bulbs to fill out your area based on the planting distances for the particular type of bulb.

If you want your bulb plantings to look natural, arrange them in an informal design. Toss bulbs randomly onto the planting bed, and then plant them where they fall. You may have to adjust them slightly to maintain correct spacing, but the effect will not be as contrived as if you tried to arrange them.

Bulbs can also be *naturalized* into an informal look, particularly appropriate in woodland settings. Bulbs can be planted to look natural and then left to multiply on their own to increase the colony. If you want to achieve this effect, select a spot for your naturalistic planting that will not have to be disturbed until after the flowers and foliage have faded away.

After bulbs have bloomed and the foliage has died down, you will be left with empty spaces. If you interplanted bulbs with a

SPRING-FLOWERING BULBS

HEIGHTS, DEPTH OF PLANTING, AND BLOOMING TIMES

FLOWER	HEIGHT	BLOOMING TIME	DEPTH
Snowdrop	4-6"	Early spring	4"
Crocus	3-5"	Early spring	3-4"
Anemone blanda **(Windflower)**	5"	Early spring	2"
Grape hyacinth (*Muscari*)	6-10"	Early spring	3"
Early tulip	10-13"	Early spring	6"
Hyacinth	12"	Early spring	6"
Daffodil	12"	Mid-spring	6"
Darwin hybrid tulip	28"	Mid-spring	6"
Crown imperial (*Fritillaria imperialis*)	30-48"	Mid-spring	5"
Late tulip	36"	Late spring	6"
Dutch iris	24"	Late spring	4"
Allium giganteum	48"	Late spring	10"

groundcover, you have no further plans to make. In flower beds, add annuals as soon as they can be planted in spring. No harm is done to bulb plantings when you overplant them with annuals.

Summer bulbs can be integrated into the landscape, filling in spaces that need color or adding a unique look to the flower bed or border. Since summer bulbs are dug up and stored each winter, you can plant them in a different spot each year, varying your design scheme.

PLANTING SPRING-FLOWERING BULBS

Until you plant your bulbs, be sure to store them in a dark, dry, and cool (but not freezing) area so they will not grow, rot, or shrivel up. A good place to store them is in a covered box inside the garage; do not keep them inside the house, as the heat will cause them to start growing.

You can plant spring-flowering bulbs at any time in fall until the soil freezes; if you can't plant them all at once, start with the smaller, earlier-flowering bulbs.

Good soil preparation is critical to a successful bulb garden. Because bulb roots reach deep, you'll need to spade and prepare the bed to a depth of 12 inches.

The soil for all bulbs must have good drainage and aeration to prevent the bulbs and roots from rotting and to allow for pore spaces into which roots can grow. Before you plant, add organic matter equal to 25 percent of the soil volume. This material may be peat moss, compost, leaf mold, or something similar.

You can prepare holes for bulbs by one of two methods: you can either dig individual holes for each bulb with a narrow trowel or bulb planting tool, or you can dig out an entire area, put the bulbs in place, and restore the soil. The latter is the better idea if you are planting a large number of bulbs.

Although bulbs contain their first season's food supply, fertilizing fosters future growth. To encourage root growth, add phosphorus-rich bonemeal to the bottom of each planting hole and place the bulb on top of it.

If squirrels, chipmunks, or other small animals are a problem in your area and tend to breakfast on your bulbs, place the bulbs in a wire basket or cage and plant them inside this protection. Another method of keeping animals from digging up bulbs is to spread chicken wire on top of the bed after it's planted. Secure the wire at the corners, and cover it with mulch.

After planting, water the beds well and mulch them with oak leaves, bark chips, or other organic mulch. One watering should be sufficient until growth starts the following spring. In spring, remove the mulch, especially from low-growing varieties, as soon as you see growth starting. Leaving mulch on too long in the spring will cause foliage to yellow and may smother the flowers of low-growing varieties.

CARING FOR SPRING-FLOWERING BULBS

Spring flowering bulbs are about the easiest of garden plants to care for. Care requirements are minimal once planted, although a few chores in the springtime will keep bulbs at their blooming best.

Even though you properly prepared your bulb bed at planting time, you will need to add extra fertilizer each year to keep the bulbs healthy and flowering at their peak. When bulb foliage begins to emerge in spring, sprinkle fertilizer on the ground and water it in. For maximum results, feed again as the foliage starts to yellow. Use either an all-purpose fertilizer, such as 5-10-5, or a specially prepared bulb food.

Once bulbs start to poke their way through the ground in spring, they will need a lot of moisture, so water deeply if spring rains do not fall. Proper flowering and growth depend on sufficient water reaching deep into the root zone.

When tulips, daffodils, hyacinths, and other large bulbs have finished blooming, cut off the flowers to prevent seed formation and to direct energy to the bulb. Smaller bulbs can be left to go to seed, which will scatter and increase the colony.

After blooms fade, bulb foliage must be left to mature if you want the bulbs to bloom again the following spring. Never remove leaves until they have completely browned and pull away from the plant easily. When bulbs are planted in a lawn, do not mow the grass until the foliage has browned.

Summer-Flowering Bulbs in the Landscape

Summer-flowering bulbs (which actually can be bulbs, tubers, rhizomes, roots, or corms) are less hardy than their springtime cousins. Because they are sensitive to freezing temperatures, such tender bulbs must be planted in the spring and dug up each fall to be stored over the winter.

Summer bulbs are the perfect addition to the flower garden. They combine perfectly with annuals and perennials, offering a color, flower form, or uniqueness that completes the scene. Many summer bulbs have exotic shapes or colors.

Where a splash of red, green, pink, silver, or white is needed, fancy-leaved *Caladium* does the trick. *Canna* also has dramatic foliage and height along with its bright flowers, making it the plant of choice if you need an accent.

Gladioluses make spectacular cut flowers. Their dramatic spikes can be grown en masse in a cutting garden or a mixed border. And, for color all summer long in the sun — whether for beds, borders, or cut flowers — dahlias are wonderful.

Formal and frilly, rose-, camellia-, or carnation-like flowers, in a painter's palette of colors — all these descriptions fit tuberous begonias. Perfect to brighten the shade, tuberous begonias do well in pots, hanging baskets, edgings, borders, and atop low walls. Often grown as houseplants, calla lilies also do well outside in partial shade.

In the genus *Anemone* are members which sport large

poppy-like flowers. They make excellent cut flowers, and add very bright colors to the early summer. Paper-like swirls of petals make *Ranunculus* (buttercups) appear too perfect to be real. For good companionship, join them up with the fragrant, colorful, and multiflowered stems of trumpet-shaped freesia.

Several other lily-like bulbs can add an exotic look to the garden, including montbretia, gloriosa lily, and acidanthera. For other "unusual" touches, intermingle blue agapanthus with tricornered tigridia (or "tiger flower").

PLANTING SUMMER BULBS

Soil with excellent drainage is required for summer-flowering bulbs. Before planting each spring, be sure the soil is rich in organic matter and well prepared. Work the soil several inches deeper than the planting depth of the bulb.

Large bulbs should be planted individually. Smaller bulbs look better planted in clumps for a massed effect. Be sure to plant at correct depths.

All summer bulbs like to be watered deeply and often. If possible, apply water to the soil, not to the foliage or blooms, to prolong flowering and keep disease to a minimum. A mulch of organic material about 2 to 3 inches thick conserves moisture and keeps roots cool as temperatures climb. Summer bulbs benefit from heavy feeding with a balanced fertilizer.

All summer bulbs need to be lifted from the ground and stored over the winter, as they cannot withstand freezing temperatures. Tuberous begonias are best dug up before the first fall frost. Others should remain in the ground until the foliage is blackened by frost. Be careful when digging not to cut or damage the roots, corms, tubers, or bulbs.

After digging up bulbs, wash off as much soil as possible with a gentle spray of water, then dry them in a sunny spot for several days. Store bulbs in a dark, dry area at 40° to 50°F. A good method of storage is in dry sphagnum peat moss in a plastic bag.

Check the bulbs often to make sure they are in good condition. If they have started to grow, they need a cooler spot. If they have started to rot, allow the packing material to dry out somewhat.

If your summer bulbs need dividing, do it in the spring just prior to planting. Cut roots and tubers with a sharp knife, making sure that each division contains at least one growing shoot or eye. True bulbs and corms produce offsets, called *bulblets* or *cormels,* which can be pulled from the parent and planted separately. They may not bloom during their first year of growth, but in time they will mature to full size.

SUMMER-FLOWERING BULBS

HEIGHTS, DATES AND DEPTHS OF PLANTING, AND SPACING

Flower	Height	Planting Time	Depth	Spacing
Acidanthera	20'	Early spring	2"	5"
Anemone (de Caen, St. Brigid)	18"	South—Sept.-Jan. North—Early spring	2"	3"
Dahlia large varieties dwarf varieties	48" 12"	After last frost	4" 4"	24" 6"
Galtonia	40"	April-May	5"	10"
Gladiolus Large-flowering Small-flowering	60" 30"	April—mid-June	3-4" 3-4"	6" 6"
Lily	3-7'	Fall or early spring	8"	8"
Montbretia	24"	April—end of May	4"	4"
Ranunculus	12"	South—Sept.-Jan.	2"	8"
Tigridia	16"	Early spring	3"	6"

CHAPTER 7
LANDSCAPING WITH ANNUALS

Instant beauty, spectacular and diverse color: these are the advantages and charms of annual flowers. By definition, an annual is a plant that grows, flowers, sets seed, and dies in the same season. The term "annual" is also applied to tender perennials that survive the winter only in the mildest of climates but are grown during the summer in other areas. The real connotations of the term "annual" though, suggest a myriad of colors, sizes, forms, and beauties, bursting forth in the landscape from spring frost to fall frost. Every year, there's the anticipation of a new look and new colors, with flowers that are readily available at minimum cost.

BEDS OR BORDERS?

The impact that flowers make is the real measure of professionalism in the home landscape. Wherever space permits, annual flower beds and/or borders should be included in the overall design. *Beds* are those plantings that are accessible from all sides. An example is an island planting in the middle of the lawn. *Borders*, on the other hand, are at the edge of an area, be it the lawn, driveway, foundation, shrub planting, or fence.

Because borders can usually be worked from only one side, do not make them any deeper than 5 feet at the most, or maintenance will be difficult. Up to that point, they can be as wide as space and looks permit. Beds should be planned in relation to the surrounding area; don't try to situate too large a bed in a small grassed area, or it will be out of proportion.

You can locate beds and borders anywhere on your grounds, uniting plantings of evergreens and flowering trees and shrubs with ribbons of living color.

Besides adding aesthetic value, beds and borders can be used to either highlight or camouflage areas or even to direct foot traffic. If you want to draw attention to your front door, frame it with color. If you want to conceal your trash cans, let an annual vine climb on a trellis in front of them. If you don't want the children cutting across the front lawn, plant a border of annuals to make them walk around the lawn to the path.

71

Special Effects with Annuals

In addition to their primary use in beds and borders, bedding plants can be called upon for a variety of special uses. Flowering vines are unequalled as temporary screens on fences, trellises, or arbors. Select from morning glory, black-eyed Susan vine, cardinal climber, moonflower, sweet pea, scarlet runner bean, or nasturtium.

In newly planted landscapes, annuals can be used as a "quick cover" while you wait for the shrubs and permanent groundcovers to mature. Depending on the exposure and temperature, a number of good choices are available. For example, in hot climates, choose vinca, portulaca, petunia, or sweet alyssum. In cool areas, select phlox or lobelia.

You may want to bring the beauty of your garden indoors and have cut flowers for the living room. Your flowering annuals can do double duty if you choose types that can be cut and used in arrangements. Frequent cutting of flowers encourages new growth as well as increased bloom.

Think of annuals as combination plants. While magnificent when used alone, they can also be planted quite effectively with perennials, summer bulbs, and dwarf shrubs. Consider rotating annual plantings over the growing season for the longest-lasting color effect. In warm areas, this can be done year-round. Start with pansies, forget-me-nots, or other cool-weather plants in the spring, followed by any of a large selection of summer annuals, and end the season with other cool favorites such as flowering mums or flowering cabbage or kale.

Designing Your Annual World

Design is the first step in creating your colorful world. Decide which plant sizes will best conform to the surroundings. Small beds or edgings along low hedges or beneath foundation plantings demand a low-growing choice, such as ageratum, alyssum, or begonias. In larger areas, you can vary the height to make the effect more interesting, especially if the ground is flat. In a free-standing bed, place taller plants in the center, stepping down to an intermediate-sized plant and then to a ground-hugging annual in front. For a border against a fence or wall, use the tallest in the back and work down to the front.

For a mixed bed or border, choose three sizes of plants. This can be done by combining three varieties of the same plant, such as zinnias or marigolds, that have different heights; or by combining three different plants, such as tall spider flowers (cleome) and medium-sized dahlias, trimmed with a carpet of low-growing petunias.

Plants grow in many different shapes, a mixture of which is most attractive in a mixed bed. Imagine a combination of spiked snapdragons intermingled with mounded begonias and edged with low-growing lobelia. Annuals can grow upright and bushy (like African marigolds) or in an open, informal manner (like cosmos). Again, try to work in groups of three.

Flowers also come in different shapes, and combining them will make a mixed bed or border much more interesting. Examples could be plumes of celosia, globes of gaillardia, trumpet-shaped petunias, and a broad assortment of single, double, round, frilled, or irregularly shaped flowers.

Although combinations are most attractive, they are not a design necessity; mass planting of one variety of impatiens, for example, in one shape or color, is just as appealing. The decision depends on the effect you want to achieve; a massed planting is sleek and modern in appearance. If the ground is flat, building berms (mounds of soil) for mass plantings will give them height and more perspective.

When you shop for bedding plants or seeds, you will notice that many annuals come in a "series." For example, there are 'Super Elfin Pink', 'Super Elfin Red', and 'Super Elfin Blush' impatiens; 'Pink Pearl', 'Azure Pearl', and 'White Pearl' petunias; and 'Inca Yellow', 'Inca Gold', and 'Inca Orange' marigolds. If you are planning a massed bed of the same plant in mixed colors, you will achieve greater success if you use plants from the same series. They will be more uniform in height, plant shape, and bloom size.

If space is tight, plant in areas that are most visible. For example, plant annual beds or borders along the walkway or driveway to greet you when you come home, or place them in the backyard, where you will be relaxing on weekends.

The shape of the planting area should be influenced by the surroundings. A stately Georgian or very modern house would demand a formal, straight-lined bed. A Colonial home would call for a closely packed, cottage-garden style. Most of today's architecture is complemented by semiformal, contoured flower beds or borders.

Growing the Annual Garden
Soil

No matter how well you plan your garden or how high the quality of your plants, you will not succeed without a good foundation: a proper soil. Before planting, you should prepare the soil, especially if a flower bed has never before been in the location where the planting will be done. After laying out the area, remove all grass, weeds, stones, and other debris.

Incorporate organic matter such as peat moss, leaf mold, or compost at a rate of about 25 percent of soil volume into the area where the roots will be growing, which is approximately the top 8 inches of soil. Fertilizer should also be mixed in; choose a kind whose ratio of nitrogen-phosphorus-potassium (N-P-K) is 1-1-1 or 1-2-1, and apply according to label directions. Spade, rototill, or otherwise mix the soil well until it is uniform. Then level it off.

Soil for most annuals should be slightly acid to neutral, with a pH of 5.5 to 7.0. Have your soil's pH tested by your County Extension Service, or test it yourself with a soil-test kit.

Beds should not be worked in the early spring when the soil is still wet, or the texture will be ruined. Build up the beds the previous fall, or in the spring just before planting.

PLANTING

If you purchase bedding plants instead of growing your own annuals from seeds, look for deep green, healthy plants that are neither too compact nor too spindly. It is better if they are not yet in bloom. Most annuals will come into full bloom faster in the garden if they are not in bloom when planted.

Most bedding plants are grown in individual "cell packs," although they may be in flats or individual pots. If you can't plant them right away, keep them in a lightly shaded spot and be sure to water them as needed. Just before planting, the bedding plants should be well watered, as should the soil in the bed or border.

Do not try to jump the gun at planting time! Tender annuals cannot be planted until after all danger of frost has passed and the soil is warm. Half-hardy annuals can be safely planted if nights are still cool, as long as there is no more danger of frost. Hardy and very hardy plants can be planted in early spring as soon as the soil can be worked.

When planting time has come, be sure to plant annuals the recommended distance apart. Beds will not look full when first planted, but the new plants will soon grow to fill the spaces.

Carefully lift plants from their cell packs or pots, keeping the root balls intact in order to avoid damage. The best way to do this is to either gently squeeze or push up the bottom of the container, if it is pliable enough, or turn it upside down to have the plant fall into your hand. If the plant does not slide out easily, tap the bottom of the container with a trowel. If the root ball is moist, as it should be, it should slip out easily without being disturbed.

Occasionally, you will find plants in a flat without individual cells. If you do, just before planting separate the plants gently by hand or with a knife, so that the roots do not dry out. Other times, plants may be growing in individual peat pots. In this case, either peel most of the pot away, or be sure the top of the pot is below soil level after planting, to prevent the plant from drying out.

If pots are extremely compacted, loosen them gently before planting. Dig a hole slightly larger than the root ball, set the plant in place at the same level at which it was growing, and carefully firm the soil around the roots. Water well soon after planting, and frequently after that, until the plants are established and new growth has started. At that time, an application of soluble fertilizer high in phosphorus will encourage root growth.

To reduce transplanting shock, plant on a cloudy or overcast day, late in the afternoon. Petunias are the most notable exception to this rule, since they tolerate planting even on hot and sunny days.

To reduce maintenance needs, use black plastic as a method of weed prevention. Be sure to punch numerous holes into the plastic with a garden rake to ensure adequate water penetration. A thin layer of decorative bark mulch will hide the plastic.

Keeping the Garden Colorful

Fertilizing

Most annuals do not require much fertilizing, but will do much better if adequate nutrients are available. Notable exceptions are nasturtium, spider flower, portulaca, amaranthus, cosmos, gazania, and salpiglossis, all of which like to be grown in poor, infertile soils. With these plants, the fertilizer incorporated before planting is adequate. With other annuals, you can fertilize once or twice during the growing season with 5-10-5 fertilizer, at the rate of 1 to 2 pounds per 100 square feet. As an alternative, you might use a soluble fertilizer such as 20-20-20, following label directions and applying every four to six weeks. Be careful, though, since overfertilizing can cause a buildup of soluble salts in the soil, and can also result in heavy foliage growth and few flowers.

Watering

Generally, heavy but infrequent watering encourages deep root growth, so annuals should be watered only as often as the lawn. Refer to seed packets or experts at garden centers for watering guidelines for specific species.

Keep the foliage dry during watering. Using soaker hoses is a good way to achieve this. However, if overhead sprinklers must be used, you should water as early in the day as possible those annuals that are disease-prone (zinnias, calendula, grandiflora petunias, and stock in particular), so that the foliage will dry out before nightfall, lessening the chances of disease.

When you use annuals for cut flowers, not watering them overhead will prevent water damage to the blooms. Where dry soil and dry skies prevail and irrigation is not possible, choose a drought-resistant annual such as portulaca, celosia, cosmos, sunflower, amaranthus, candytuft, dusty miller, gazania, spider flower, sweet alyssum, or vinca.

Mulching

After your annuals are planted, adding a 2- to 3-inch layer of mulch will not only add a note of attractiveness, it will also reduce weeds and conserve soil moisture, resulting in better growth. The best mulches are organic, and include bark chips, pine needles, shredded leaves, peat moss, or hulls of some kind. The following year, the mulch can be incorporated into the soil before planting, thereby enriching it. Additional mulch can be added each spring, resulting in better soil structure and therefore better growth as years pass.

Weeding

In addition to supplying the basic requirements for good growth, you will want to weed your plants in order to keep beds and borders as appealing as possible. Weeds may appear even if you mulch. Be sure to remove weeds as soon as possible, so that they do not compete with the flowers for water and nutrients. Remove weeds carefully, especially when the annuals are young, so you do not disturb the annuals' roots.

CHAPTER 8

FOUNDATION PLANTING WITH PERENNIALS

There was a time when no one would think of buying anything but tightly clipped evergreens for foundation plants around the home. Not anymore. Flowering shrubs and planters filled with annuals are now popular, and many homeowners also use perennial flowers for this purpose — they are far less expensive than shrubbery and easier to bring home and plant.

The best perennials to use near a house are those that will develop into good-sized plants, but not spread out too much. Because they are always on display, they should have attractive foliage and look nice even when not in bloom. You could, for example, use several varieties and heights of daylilies for this purpose, as well as large clumps of pink peonies. Hostas are excellent, especially for shady spots, and the aromatic *Dictamnus* (gas plant) also works well in the shade. Plants such as *Dicentra spectabilis* (old-fashioned bleeding-heart), lupines, delphinium, and Oriental poppies are all attractive when they're in bloom, but look sad after their blossoming period is finished and the foliage has died back. If you use them, do it sparingly, and tuck in tall-growing annuals or brightly colored geraniums to camouflage their messy post-bloom foliage.

If your building is white, brown, gray, or another neutral shade, you will not need to be fussy about choosing flowering plants of the proper color; but if it is red, blue, yellow, or an unusual tone, select plants that will have compatible blooms. Those with pale or white blossoms may, in some cases, be your best option.

You can plant large clumps of the more massive perennials just as you would evergreens or flowering shrubs, with tall ones at the corners and on each side of the front doorways, and with lower-growing kinds under the windows. Or you may decide to grow a narrow perennial border or cottage garden next to the building instead.

If your building has wood siding, leave a space between your perennials and the structure, so the moisture-holding plants won't rot the wood or deteriorate the paint. Unless you plan to water frequently, set the perennials outside the drip line of any overhanging roof so that they will get the benefit of rainfall. The more rugged varieties of hosta and daylilies grow well even under eaves without gutters, but it is not generally advisable to set plants where they might drown in a downpour.

As with any planting, provide good topsoil, proper drainage, and a location that will provide enough sunlight. Mulch the area around the plants with bark, wood chips, or another attractive material: it will prevent rain from splashing dirt on the house, help control weeds, and conserve soil fertility. Add fertilizer a couple of times during the summer if rain from the roof is likely to wash out fertility, and add a sprinkling of lime each year for the same reason. A weed-check fabric (available from most garden supply stores) that allows moisture to penetrate, when placed under the mulch, will save a lot of weeding time.

Shaded areas that receive only a few hours of direct sunlight, but are still exposed to bright skylight for the rest of the day, are not a good spot for sun-loving plants. The best plant choices for these spots are columbine, *Dicentra eximia* (fringed bleeding-heart), ferns, hosta, daylilies, monkshood, and globeflower. For the difficult-to-grow north side of a building and other areas that get little direct sunlight try ferns, hosta, and beds of *Convallaria* (lily-of- the-valley).

PERENNIALS OFTEN USED AS FOUNDATION PLANTS

Althaea rosea, hollyhock

Chrysanthemum

Chrysanthemum maximum, Shasta daisy

Dictamnus, gas plant

Gaillardia, blanketflower

Hemerocallis, daylily

Hosta, plantain lily

Lavandula, lavender

Oenothera, evening primrose

Paeonia, peony

Phlox

Potentilla, cinquefoil

Rudbeckia hirta, gloriosa daisy